Read what others are saying about this book

"This book is so reduced, so concise, so easy to grasp—so if you're really serious about writing, grab it."
—**Barnaby Conrad, Founder and Director,**
Santa Barbara Writers Conference

"The advice contained in this book comes from those who have succeeded in their writing careers. The sensible counsel in this well-written anthology has immediate and long-term benefits for the serious writer."
—**Ray Newton, National Coordinator,**
Reader's Digest Writing Workshops

"[This book is] loaded with practical and inspirational tips for writing success."
—**Nat Bodian,** *The Book Marketing Handbook*

"The information in this book is worth thousands of dollars. Don't even think about writing or publishing a nonfiction book without it!"
—**Jack Canfield, co-author and editor**
of the best-selling *Chicken Soup for the Soul*®
series

"Dan Poynter is a wealth of publishing information. That makes what he's selected to share all that more valuable."
—**Gordon Burgett,** *Publishing to Niche Markets*

"Dan Poynter's *Successful Nonfiction* is a must read. He gives many valuable tips that can move you light-years ahead in your work. I plan to keep his book on my desk alongside my *Chicago Manual of Style* and *Roget's Thesaurus*."
—**Mary Embree, Literary Consultant and**
Founder of the Small Publishers,
Artists and Writers Network

"The main reason people don't finish their books is lack of motivation. If this book doesn't inspire you to finish your manuscript and get it into print, nothing will."
—**Robert W. Bly,** *Getting Your Book Published*

"There are not many perfect books but this is one of them. It provides two of the three 'in' words a writer needs to succeed—information and inspiration. The third is inner drive, but the writer must provide that himself. And Dan delivers it all with the greatest weapon a writer has at his disposal—fun. Dan knows how to entertain, so his reader enjoys the experience of reading."
—**John Tullius, Founder and Director,**
Maui Writers Conference

"Throw away your library of how-to-write books and grab this one. It's packed with ideas, tips and tricks to help you write and sell your book. I love it!"
—**Joe Vitale,** *There's a Customer Born Every Minute*

"I can't imagine a better gift for anyone who ever thought of writing."
—**Maryanne Raphael,** *Writers World*

"This book is a keeper with practical insights on every page. It belongs in every writer's library."
—**Terry Paulson, Ph.D., author of**
50 Tips for Speaking Like a Pro **and 1998–99**
President of the National Speakers Association

"Fun. Informative. Motivational. The perfect gift for your writer friends."
—**Dianna Booher,** *Communicate with*
Confidence, The Worth of a Woman's Words **and**
Get a Life Without Sacrificing Your Career

"Once again, Dan untiringly offers up more of his expertise and experience to the army of nonfiction warriors. This is a marvelous 'crack sealer.'"
—**Raleigh Pinskey,** *101 Ways to Promote Yourself*
and *You Can Hype Anything*

"Why settle for writing a good book when you can write a great one? This book shows how to create a great book even if it's your first. You will find wisdom on every page."
—**Terri Lonier,** *Working Solo*

Successful Nonfiction

Tips and Inspiration for Getting Published

Dan Poynter

First Edition

Para Publishing, Santa Barbara, California

Successful Nonfiction

Dan Poynter

Published by:
  Para Publishing
  Post Office Box 8206
  Santa Barbara, CA 93118-8206, U.S.A.
  info@ParaPublishing.com
  http://ParaPublishing.com

Unattributed quotations are by Dan Poynter.
Some images by Jeanette Jaramillo.
Some images copyright by http://www.arttoday.com

Library of Congress Cataloging-in-Publication Data
Poynter, Dan.
Successful nonfiction: tips and inspiration for getting published
/ Poynter, Dan. – 1st ed.
   p. cm.
   Includes bibliographical references and index.
   ISBN 1-56860-061-5
   1. Authorship. 2. Authorship—marketing. I. Title.
PN145.P64 2000
808'.02—dc21   99-41089
                              CIP

Contents

Chapter One   9
On Writing

Chapter Two   51
Why Write?

Chapter Three   63
Why a Book?

Chapter Four   69
What to Write

Chapter Five   93
Research

Chapter Six   101
Building your Book

Chapter Seven   111
Copyright

Chapter Eight   115
Finding an Agent;
Finding a Publisher

Chapter Nine   127
Book Promotion

Appendix   134
Writing Resources   135
Index   139

About the Author

Dan Poynter fell into writing. He spent eight years researching a labor of love. Realizing no publisher would be interested in a technical treatise on the parachute, he went directly to a printer and "self-published." Orders poured in and he suddenly found he was also a publisher. Since 1969, he has written 77 books, 47 special reports, 500 magazine articles, 9 audiotapes and 2 videotapes. Most of these information products focus on book writing and publishing. In the publishing field, he is widely known for his best-selling *The Self-Publishing Manual: How to Write, Print and Sell Your Own Book.*

Dan Poynter's seminars have been featured on CNN, his books have been mentioned in *The Wall Street Journal*, and his story has been told in *U.S. News & World Report*. The media come to him because he is the leading authority on nonfiction book writing, publishing and promoting.

Dan is descended from a long line of published authors including Stephen Vincent Benét, William Rose Benét, James Thompson, Frank Norris, Charles G. Norris, Kathleen Norris, Margaret Bridgman and Josephine Poynter.

A consultant to the book industry, he was recently presented with the Benjamin Franklin Award for Lifetime Achievement by the Publishers Marketing Association. Dan is a past vice-president of the PMA.

Dan is a frequent speaker at the Santa Barbara Writers Conference, the Maui Writers Conference and many other industry events. He runs his own publishing company, Para Publishing, in Santa Barbara.

Acknowledgment

I am deeply indebted to the many wonderful people from the writing trade and publishing industry mentioned in the text. In many cases, I included their web site or email address for more information.

Penny Paine monitored the quality, Gail Kearns did the content editing, Barbara Coster of Cross-t.i did the copy editing and proofreading, Jeanette Jaramillo contributed several drawings, Robert Howard provided another great cover design, and Christine Nolt of Cirrus Design is responsible for the book design and typography.

I sincerely thank all these fine people, and I know they are proud of their contributions to the book community as well as to this work.

Colophon

Manuscript written in Microsoft Word 2000.

Typesetting in QuarkXpress.

Type font: Headings in Della Robia, Text in Giovanni Book

Cover: 3.5" French flaps printed four color on 10 pt. C1S with gold foil, embossing and matte film lamination.

Endsheets: 80# natural.

Text paper: 50# Glatfelter Natural Antique, 400 PPI.

Printed by United Graphics, Mattoon, Illinois.

Disclaimer

Even great books have their limitations. (Please see page 110 on Disclaimers). This book is designed to provide information about the subject matter covered. It is sold with the understanding that the publisher and author are not engaged in rendering legal, accounting or other professional services. If expert assistance is required, the services of a competent professional should be sought.

It is not the purpose of this book to reprint all the information that is otherwise available to authors and other creative people but to complement, amplify and supplement other texts. For more information, see your bookstore.

Book writing is not a get-rich-quick scheme. Anyone who decides to write a book must expect to invest a lot of time and effort without any guarantee of success. Books do not write themselves and they do not sell themselves. Authors write and promote their books.

Every effort has been made to make this book as complete and as accurate as possible. However, there may be mistakes both typographical and in content. Therefore, this text should be used only as a general guide and not as the ultimate source of writing and publishing information. Furthermore, this book contains information on writing and publishing that is current only up to the printing date.

The purpose of this manual is to educate and entertain. The author and Para Publishing shall have neither liability nor responsibility to any person or entity with respect to any loss or damage caused or alleged to be caused directly or indirectly by the information contained in this book.

If you do not wish to be bound by the above, you may return this book to the publisher for a full refund. For those who love to find mistakes, please send your corrections for the next edition.

Chapter One
On Writing

Writing is a creative act. Building a nonfiction book requires planning, structure and lots of labor. Your intellectual property is a piece of art; it will not design itself or be created overnight.

Writing a book is a journey, a trip to be enjoyed on the way to the reward at the destination. Learning as you research your subject is stimulating. The thought process of distilling the pertinent information for your readers is invigorating. Crafting just the right words to convey your message is energizing and provides the power to maintain your writing momentum. The published book is your goal but the process is fun. You are fortunate to be a writer.

This chapter will take you through the four nonfiction drafts with dozens of tips from the best in the business:

- Rough draft
- Content edit
- Peer review
- Copy edit (including fact checking)

Writing is creative, writing is fun. Good writing begets better writing—so practice.

Write a Page-Turner
Get the reader past page eighteen.

Start your book off with an *action chapter*; make it exciting. Like the introductory part of a speech, Chapter One should arouse the reader and whet his or her appetite. Too many authors want to start from the *beginning* and describe their research or put a boring history chapter first. The reader wants to know "where to" and "how to." Do not sedate the reader in the first chapter; encourage him or her to read on.

It has been reported that most book buyers do not get past page 18 in a new book. They buy it, bring it home, begin reading, and then put it down on the bedside table. And they never get back to it. Your book has to be exciting in the initial pages to keep the reader involved and reading.

Getting a customer to buy your book is not enough. You want your buyer to read it, underline it, highlight it, talk about it, move to action and profit from it. A satisfied reader will recommend your book to friends and your fans will buy your next book.

Hit the page writing.

It is the writer's fault, not the reader's, if the reader puts down the book.
—David Halberstam, author.

Don't Allow Interruptions

God made the earth in six days and then he rested. He could have done the job in just four days if it had not been for all the interruptions.

Good writing requires concentration. Interruptions often occur when you are deep in thought and producing your best work.

Emergencies such as earthquakes, fire and flood are interruptions we can accept. We may even weave the unexpected experience into our future work. Telephone calls, visitors and unnecessary questions are interruptions that may make a writer a bit snippy. This is perfectly normal. If people do not want to hear you yell at them, they should leave you alone.

Novelist Judith Krantz places this sign on her door:

> DO NOT COME IN. DO NOT KNOCK. DO NOT SAY "HELLO." DO NOT SAY "I'M LEAVING." DO NOT SAY ANYTHING UNLESS THE HOUSE IS ON FIRE.

Explain to your family: "I love you but I am working now. Working requires concentration, and one brief interruption can cause me to lose a train of thought and lose an hour or more of time. Your brief greeting or question could cause me to lose a valuable thought that will affect our income." Set boundaries and unplug the telephone.

Sue Grafton lives in Santa Barbara. In 1993 she returned to the University of Louisville to accept an honor. On a lark, she went to look at houses—and bought one. Now she writes in both places. She says, "It's really quiet in Kentucky because no one knows when I'm there."

Writing is a solitary occupation. Family, friends and society are the natural enemies of the writer. He must be alone, uninterrupted, and slightly savage if he is to sustain and complete an undertaking.
—Lawrence Clark Powell (1906–), author.

Take Your Time

How long does it take to write a book?

That's like asking, "How much is a car?" It depends on a great many things.

When Maryanne Raphael first read about the international Three-Day Writing Contest, she thought it was a joke. But the idea of writing a book in three days fascinated her. So several years later she signed up, got a sponsor, and arranged to spend Labor Day weekend at her keyboard day and night.

She began writing as fast as she could, doing her best at all times because there was no chance for rewriting. The subconscious was in control, with the conscious mind in the dark much of the time. The same powerful curiosity that keeps readers turning pages kept her writing them.

She finished the manuscript, *The Man Who Loved Funerals*, by the deadline, with short breaks for stretching and naps. It is now in New York with her agent, who thinks it is her best work. And she has spent ten years writing her nonfiction book, *How To Write a Novel in Three Days*.

http://whitehall-realty/publish/mraphael/mother

According to Brenner Information Group, on the average, it takes 475 hours to write fiction books and 725 hours to write nonfiction.

For many authors, the *writing* of the book is a journey to be enjoyed.

You've lived 78 years and you expect me to ghostwrite your memoir in a week?
—**Gail Kearns, writer and editor.**

Allocate Time

Does your writing come first or last?

Many writers like to set aside a few hours for their writing each day; they establish a schedule and stick to it religiously. A few have the luxury of writing full-time or of getting away to concentrate on their writing. They find marathon writing is more fun and avoids the challenge of getting back to the manuscript each day. Still others have to fit in their writing whenever they can.

Nat Bodian decided to write his first book in 1979. Finding time was difficult because he worked full-time as a marketer at a New York publishing house and commuted from New Jersey. He did some writing on the bus to and from New York, some was done on a pad of paper walking across Manhattan and some was done during his lunch hours. Then, evenings after his kids were in bed, he continued in a basement typing room until the wee hours of the morning and on weekends.

The *Book Marketing Handbook* was published by R.R. Bowker 20 months later and it is still selling. This and several more industry books led to his nomination to the Publishing Hall of Fame.

NatBodian@aol.com

Subscribers to *Writer's Digest* magazine spend 12.64 hours writing each week. Beginners spend 7 hours a week and advanced writers spend 30.5.

Mahatma Gandhi and Martin Luther King Jr. wrote powerful articles and books about their activities or causes while behind bars. Make effective use of your most valuable asset: your time.

Writing has to come first.
—Sue Grafton, author, "O" Is for Outlaw.

Overcome Writer's Block

If you wait for inspiration, you are a waiter, not a writer.

If you are having trouble getting started, look at other books. Go to the bookstore, library, and surf the Web. See what is available on your topic (and what is not). Read about writing and about your subject. More research will give you more ideas.

Paul and Sarah Edwards, the nation's "self-employment experts" and authors of eight books, say, "We nonfiction writers do not get classic writer's block. We get brain block. We get disconnected from what we have to say. So, when you get stuck, ask yourself, 'What do I have to say about this?' or 'What do people need to know?' Then start writing down whatever comes to mind.

"If you draw a complete blank, check out what others think about the topic by reading what they have written or doing a few interviews. Then write out what you think about what you have heard or read. What conclusions have you reached? Do you agree or disagree? Is your experience similar or different?

"What are others overlooking? What can you add? Write it all down and you are underway.

"When you have difficulty writing, try talking. Talk about what you would like to say. Tape it if that will help you remember. Then write down what you just said."

http://www.paulandsarah.com

If you can't seem to write just now, do something for your book, anything. Exercise your mind; take your brain for a *book walk*. Go somewhere either book- or subject-related.

To overcome writer's block, get something—anything—down on paper. Don't wait for perfection to issue forth. Since the key to good writing is rewriting, give yourself something to edit.
—James Freund, author, Smart Negotiating: How to Make Good Deals in the Real World.

Respect Your Reader's Time

Time is not money. Today, most consumers have more money than time.

Your reader wants your information but must fit it into a busy schedule.

Everyone is trying to save time. The need for speed has given rise to McDonald's, Fed Ex and Kinko's. In fact, more food goes out the side window at McDonald's than through the front door. McDonald's is a "drive-through" restaurant. Diners not only want fast food, they do not have time to sit down at a table to eat it.

Many people save time by doing two or more things at once. You can see them on the freeway, driving, eating, talking on the phone and combing their hair—all at the same time.

Research, compile the information, and condense it down to just the nuggets. Do your best for your reader by writing the solution to his or her challenges in as few words as possible.

Use brief wording and paragraphs. Your reader wants the information; he or she is not reading your nonfiction book to be diverted.

The writer does the most who gives his reader the most knowledge and takes from him the least time.
—Charles Caleb Colton, *Lacon*, 1825.

Be Precise

Cut out the 'fuzz' in fuzzy writing.

It is easy to ramble and be fuzzy; tight, precise writing is hard to do.

Ray Newton, National Coordinator of the Reader's Digest Writing Workshops, says, "If you think about the following guidelines the next time you write, you will eliminate the fuzz and lint that clutters sentences and paragraphs.

- Write short sentences.
- Have one idea in a sentence.
- Use active, not passive voice.
- Avoid using prepositional phrases when you can.
- Put subjects and verbs at the beginning of sentences.
- Avoid jargon, clichés and hackneyed expressions."

Tourism.Research@nau.edu

Examine your writing critically. Reviewers and readers will. Write in a clear and meaningful manner.

I prefer to underwrite. Simple, clear as a country creek.
—Truman Capote, novelist.

Learn to Sell

Writing a book is a creative act.
A finished book is a product.
Selling a book is a business.

Some writers feel that they are creative people and do not want to dirty their hands with the crass commercialism of selling their wares. Wake up! Your book has to be sold—many times.

Dan Millman (*Way of the Peaceful Warrior* and *Body Mind Mastery*) reminds us: "Amateur writers may have exceptional skills and talent, but they write for self-expression. Professional writers know they are creating a product to sell in the literary marketplace—a product that has to appeal to enough people who are willing to exchange money for words.

"Your book is not sold just once; it has to be sold up to eight times.

First, you sell it to yourself.

Second, you sell it to an agent.

Third, your agent sells it to an editor.

Fourth, your editor must sell it to the editorial board.

Fifth, the publisher must sell it to the sales force.

Sixth, the sales force needs to sell it to the stores.

Seventh comes the final glorious sale—to your readers.

Eighth, your readers will sell it by word of mouth to other readers."

http://www.DanMillman.com

To become a professional writer, you need to be good at what you do and you need to be good at *selling* what you do.

When you market your writing, you are in sales. Think accordingly. Act accordingly.
—Paul Raymond Martin, author, The Writer's Little Instruction Book.

Combat Procrastination

Emmett's Law: The dread of doing a task uses up more time and energy than doing the task itself.

The writing project was going so smoothly it was scary. Rita Emmett started at the top in approaching a literary agent, and her first choice accepted her. The book, with a working title of *The Complete Procrastinator's Handbook*, was a user-friendly, fun approach to helping people conquer procrastination. She sent off a rough draft of the manuscript to her agent, and it was returned with suggestions for a format, plus instructions that Rita polish it and return it as soon as possible.

Then the winds of change tornadoed Rita's life. Family illness, death of a loved one and marriages of her children sent her life spinning, so she decided to "put the book on the back burner" while she concentrated on these more important life events.

It was not procrastination, it was a choice, a priority—and that was reasonable. But she never communicated this decision to her agent—and that was inexcusable.

Three years later, Rita's life finally settled down. It was time to return to the book. She could not not do it. Although the contract had expired, she felt—morally and ethically—that she should give her agent the choice of working with her or not. More than that, she really *wanted* to work with the agent. But Rita was too embarrassed about the lapsed time, and she dreaded making that phone call. Thus began a year of procrastination—phony excuses, being too busy, *anything* to put that phone call as far from her mind as possible. The irony of putting off a book about procrastination was too painful to talk about. It added to her embarrassment.

The day came when the dread of making that phone call was making Rita sick. She had hit bottom and she finally decided to summon her courage and use every trick in the book—*her* book—to make that call. The agent courteously listened to her and graciously offered to look at her new manuscript. Rita's procrastination had ended.

The agent found a publisher, negotiated a wonderful advance, and that's the end of that story—and the beginning of Rita's life as an author—and as a recovering procrastinator.

Remmett312@aol.com

Just do it.

I have never met an author who was sorry he or she wrote a book. They are only sorry they did not write it sooner.
—**Sam Horn, speaker, author,** *Tongue Fu.*

Write Your Very Best

Good work keeps readers coming back.

You are a professional. Readers are paying good money, and they expect good work. It is poor reasoning to save your best writing for a future piece. Each reader deserves your best.

Dianna Booher submitted her 318-page manuscript titled *Executive's Portfolio of Model Speeches* to Prentice Hall. As is their typical policy, the editor sent the manuscript to their review committee before final acceptance. After their review, she received a letter from the editor asking for new ideas for her next book and commending her on the quality of the manuscript.

Along with his letter, the editor attached a letter from his review team of freelance editors and academicians. One commented that he had been a freelance editor for the major publishers for 25 years and had never worked on a manuscript that was "so clean and of such high quality." He and the editorial committee had only three issues/questions they felt the Prentice Hall editor should discuss with Dianna before sending the manuscript off to the production people. (1) They wanted to know why she had quoted so many more male Fortune 500 CEOs in the book than females. (Her answer: "There are more male CEOs to select from.") (2) They questioned the accuracy of a quotation because of its odd phrasing. (Her response: "I double-checked and my version is correct.") (3) Why had she decided to quote from Roger Smith, former CEO of GM, while he was in such disfavor? (Her response: "He is still a worthy voice on my subject.")

The freelance editor's letter went on to close after summarizing these three issues: "Given the quality of this manuscript, however, we as a committee are sure this author had good reason for using the Roger Smith quotation, so we would suggest leaving it in regardless of the current news flap."

Dianna's acquiring editor still calls her after all these years asking her if she might be interested in doing other books for them.

http://www.booherconsultants.com

Writing is a learning experience; both your writing and material will improve with practice. Give your best effort and there will be another book and another. Turn out a superior book and your agent, publisher and readers will eagerly wait for the next one.

The reward for work well done is the opportunity to do more.
**—Jonas Salk, physician and epidemiologist who
developed the first polio vaccine.**

Make Your Writing Compelling
The written word should be powerful.

Your nonfiction should not only inform, it should move your reader to action. Too much writing explains how to do something but it does not motivate the reader to do it.

In June 1999, three Jewish synagogues in Sacramento, California, were firebombed early on a Friday morning. Two of the structures received relatively minor damage, but the third attack destroyed the 5,000-volume library at B'nai Israel. The library had been the treasure of the congregation.

That night, the Friday Sabbath Service was held in the 2,000-seat community theater. More than 1,800 people of all faiths attended to show support. The United Methodist Church was holding a convention in town. When they heard of the firebombing, they decided to attend the Jewish service—and they took up a special offering. The Methodists presented a check for $6,000. Initially, the audience was stunned and silent; then they broke into continuous applause.

Author-publisher Alan Canton was so deeply moved that he wrote the story eloquently and posted it to some book-publishing listservs and newsgroups on the Internet. Readers were so motivated that they sent money and forwarded the story on to other book friends. The message spread around the world at the speed of email. Envelopes and checks poured in at the rate of 200 and 300 per day. Three months later, Canton had collected over $200,000.

http://www.adams-blake.com

The pen is mightier than the sword.
> **—Edward George Bulwer-Lytton, English novelist, dramatist and politician, in *Richelieu* (1839).**

Make Your Book Worth the Money

Size matters.

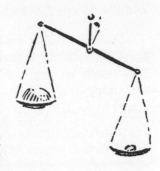

If your book is under 100 pages, it will not command the price you must get for your work. But do not pad your work with unnecessary extra writing.

To lengthen your book, add resources to the appendix: list other relevant books, videos, courses, mailing lists, associations, suppliers, etc. Now your book becomes a valuable reference.

Other ways to lengthen the book—while making it more valuable and more interesting—is to add quotations, stories and illustrations to the pages and/or summaries at the end of each chapter. Be sure to lay out the pages with plenty of white space.

Leigh Cohn took three of his wife's 30-page pamphlets on bulimia and combined them into a single book. They added resources, a two-week program to stop bingeing and a guide for support groups. Lindsey Hall's 160-page *Bulimia: A Guide to Recovery* has been through five revised editions for more than 100,000 copies in print.

Since then, they have written nine books, established their own publishing company with more than 20 titles currently in print, launched an eating disorder resource catalog and published a clinical newsletter.

http://www.gurze.com

I hope you got as much out of reading my book as I got spending the money you paid for it.
—Anonymous

Get Editorial & Design Help

Savvy authors get help.

Do not try to do it all yourself; get a support team behind you. Hire professionals.

Gordon Burgett used to do everything himself. He did the writing, content editing, copy editing, typesetting, proofreading, order taking, invoicing, shipping and even sweeping. Today, he employs professional editors, proofreaders, typesetters, cover artists and office staff. Some are subcontracted and some are full-time.

Gordon gets help, not because he is lazy but because these experts and professionals help him produce a better book.

http://www.sops.com

Editors and other book professionals are a good investment. They contribute their years of experience and expertise to your project. They can save you from mistakes and polish your work. They are worth their weight in gold.

http://www.parapublishing.com/getpage.cfm?file=/supplier.html&userid=10228333

The man of science appears to be the only man who has something to say just now—and the only man who does not know how to say it.
—Sir James Barrie (1860–1937), Scottish dramatist and novelist.

Know When to Call a Ghostwriter

You do not have to be a writer to be an author.

According to a recent *New York Times* article, "On any given week, up to a half of the books on any nonfiction best-seller list are written by someone other than the name on the book." The reason is simple: being an expert, an eyewitness or a celebrity does not necessarily mean that one is also a skilled writer/communicator. Enter the ghostwriter.

Ghosts typically work for four kinds of clients. One is the expert, who writes to preserve and share his or her knowledge. Another has an extraordinary first-person experience to relate. The third is a celebrity or aspiring celebrity who wants a book to memorialize or launch a career. The fourth has a fictional story to tell, but not the necessary storytelling skills.

Do you think Lee Iacocca wrote those two best-selling books all by himself? Iacocca is the *author*; it is his information, but he does not have time to be a *writer*.

The ghostwriter fills in for any skill or knowledge that the author lacks. In return for their expertise, ghosts are typically paid a cash fee plus a percentage of the author's royalties. In return, the ghost takes a vow of perpetual silence.

If you are not a fully skilled writer, but have expert knowledge or an extraordinary experience to share, or seek to launch or enhance your image, that's when you should call a ghostwriter.

Writing is the toughest thing I've ever done.
—Richard M. Nixon, 37th President of the United States.

Get Rolling in the Rough

The First Draft: Rough *is not ready.*

To first-draft your book, take one (chapter) pile of notes, string them out on your desk in some semblance of order, and type as fast as you can. Do not be concerned about punctuation, grammar or style at this point. Just get your notes and research materials into the machine. You will edit the text later.

As you draft each chapter of your book, run a quick spell check, print it out and place it in a three-ring binder.

Weldon Vlasak, D.Sc., began his book by drafting the introduction. It wasn't right so he rewrote it. Then he rewrote it again. Several edits later, he still was not satisfied. His lack of progress was defeating. Looking at the book from the beginning and not sure where it was going, he could not continue; he was not getting anywhere.

Four months later, he returned to the project by drafting a fascinating chapter—then another chapter and another. Finally he returned to the introduction and the words flowed. *The Secret of Gravity and Other Mysteries of the Universe* was born and broke new ground.

adaptent@naix.net

Do not edit any of the chapters until you rough draft the entire book. If you write, edit, re-edit and polish each chapter before going to the next, you will never make noticeable progress. As you place each chapter into the binder, you will gain a great feeling of accomplishment. And do not start writing at the beginning of the book.

The beautiful part of writing is that you don't have to get it right the first time, unlike, say, a brain surgeon.
—Robert Cormier, novelist.

Fill in the Blanks

The Second Draft is your content edit.

Once the first draft is in the binder, you have quantified your writing project. Some areas are not complete; some thoughts are just a reminding note. Now you can see what needs to be done. It is time to do more research: Get on the Web, return to the library, call resource people and ask questions. It is time to fill in the blanks.

When I was researching the first book on hang gliding (my third book), there was very little known about this emerging sport. Living on the East Coast at the time, I exhausted all the information sources available to me. As I drafted the text, I made a list of questions and another list of needed photographs. Then I flew to Southern California where the sport was much more advanced. Through interviews, I found answers to my questions and I purchased photographs from some noted hang gliding photographers. I took additional photos myself.

If you love your subject, the content edit can be fun. You get to conduct research and fill in the blanks.

> *The second draft is the updraft—you fix it up. You try to say what you want to say more accurately.*
> **—Anne Lamott, author, Bird by Bird.**

Writing is All About Rewriting
And rewriting and rewriting . . .

Writing a good book is not just a matter of having a good idea. Nor is it a matter of just putting your good idea down on paper. More often than not, it is about the very trying process of rewriting and tightening the manuscript—and then rewriting and tightening it again. Herein lies the hazard.

The trick in rewriting is to make your manuscript better, not worse. Rewriting portions of text too many times can cause the words to lose their spontaneity and become wooden. The writing becomes dull and unimpassioned.

Editor Gail Kearns has worked with book writers and screenwriters who can spit out a draft of a screenplay or manuscript as fast as lightning, but when it comes to the rewrite, they are stopped dead in their tracks. She says, "It is almost as if they used up all their creativity on that first draft. Then it becomes a tug of war to come up with new ideas."

The rewrite and tightening process involves choosing better words, clarifying thoughts and cutting repetition. "When in doubt, cut it out." For many writers, this is easier said than done because they become overly attached to their words. It can be like asking a child to let go of his or her favorite toy. Not easy.

There are days when the result is so bad that no fewer than five revisions are required. In contrast, when I'm greatly inspired, only four revisions are needed.
—**John Kenneth Galbraith, economist, author,**
The Affluent Society.

Know What to Cut

Write tightly.

The value of a book is in the weight of its message, not in its number of pages. Ask the three magic questions of every sentence, paragraph and word:

First, can this be written more aptly?

Second, can this be written more briefly?

Third, do I need to write this at all?

Andrea Glass is not only on a perpetual diet to lose weight, she is always seeking to cut the fat out of her writing. She has found the best way to practice writing tightly is to select a project with a word limit and stick to the rules "like the fat does to my bones." When she cuts a 1,500-word article down to 1,000 words, it is invariably so much better. Doing this has greatly assisted her in discovering where she has been excessively verbose, using needless adjectives and adverbs instead of powerhouse nouns and verbs. "Just as I prepare to fit into those size eight jeans I haven't worn for years, my lean writing fits into magazines, newsletters, brochures and this fine book!"
AndreaGlass@juno.com

Write tightly. As Elmore Leonard says, "Cut out those parts that people skip over." Shorter is better. Less is most often more. Know what to cut—and cut it.

I made this letter longer than usual because I lack the time to make it short.
—Blaise Pascal (1623–1662), French philosopher, mathematician and physicist.

Be Careful of Collaborations

Do not collaborate with someone you would not go camping with.

Writing a book with a co-author is usually a very close relationship. You are not two independent writers placing your work between the same covers. Each of you is drafting sections or chapters and exchanging them so that the other may edit and add content.

Some authors work best alone; they find that a co-author slows them down. But Maryanne Raphael loves working in collaboration. Maybe it is because she began writing before she learned to read, so she had to have a collaborator, her grandfather, who typed her stories as she dictated them. The first story they submitted was called "Pray for the Wanderer." It was not too long before Maryanne got her first rejection slip—at age five. Fortunately, she persisted.

Thirty years later, when Maryanne told a Catholic nun the story, Sister Roberta said, "Oh, I have a wonderful story about Wanderers." This time Sister Roberta dictated the story and Maryanne typed it, tightening and adding a few items. They mailed it to *Catholic Digest*, which published it under both of their names. Sister Roberta had taken a vow of poverty so she insisted Maryanne keep the entire check. No wonder Maryanne loves to collaborate.

http://whitehall-realty/publish/mraphael/mother

Collaborations are easy to get into and hard to get out of. Most business partnerships have about the same track records as marriages. A marital divorce is hard on the kids. A collaboration divorce is hard on the book. Some authors may be better off hiring a content editor or a ghostwriter. See *Is There a Book Inside You?* (Appendix, page 135).

> *I've always believed in writing without a collaborator, because where two people are writing the same book, each believes he gets all the worries and only half the royalties.*
> —**Agatha Christie, English mystery writer.**

Use Email

Save time.

Email is one of the best tools available to writers. By speeding up your correspondence, you will often get answers while the thought is still fresh in your mind. You can even use it to collaborate.

Joel Jacobs and Michael Sedge often discussed collaborating on a book, but then Joel moved to Texas and Michael took up residence in Italy. Within weeks, they were passing 10 to 30 messages back and forth each day. The 560-page manuscript was completed in a year.

They learned about compatible word processing programs, email programs and software versions. Text and formatting will be consistent if you use the same programs.

Finally, they sent their work via email as "attachments." They also discovered they should use the same margin settings, type styles, fonts, point sizes, etc., so they could merge their chapters into a single work.
pp10013@cybernet.it

Email will not resolve all the perils of co-authoring, but it offers a new, dynamic method to working together whether you live nearby or in different parts of the world.

Why pay the Postal Service 33 cents to store your mail?

Get Help From Experts

The Third Draft is the peer review.

Savvy nonfiction authors take each chapter of their nearly complete manuscript and send it off to at least four experts on that particular chapter's subject.

Some experts might get two or three chapters but most will get only one. Do not overwhelm them. If you send the whole manuscript, most experts will put it on their desk with the best of intentions and never get back to it.

Ken Blanchard, co-author of *The One-Minute Manager Library*, says, "I don't write my books, my friends write them for me." He explains that he jots down some ideas and sends them off to friends for comment. They send back lots of good ideas that he puts into his manuscript. Ken is being very generous, of course, and what he is describing is "peer review."

http://www.BlanchardTraining.com

What you get back from your peer reviewers is extremely valuable: They may add two more items to your list; they sometimes delete whole paragraphs where the practice has changed; they occasionally cross out that comment you thought was cute but was really embarrassingly stupid; and they sometimes even correct punctuation, grammar and style.

Also send copies of the complete manuscript off to friends, family, literate objective readers, potential buyers and even a devil's advocate or two.

When your book comes out, you will receive far less adverse readers' reactions because the book will be bulletproof. After all, it has been reviewed and accepted by the best.

And, there is another valuable reason for peer review: You have more than two dozen opinion molders telling everyone about your book—and how they helped you with it.

An expert is a man who has made all the mistakes which can be made in a very narrow field.
    —Niels Bohr (1885–1962), Danish physicist and Nobel laureate.

Keep Your Book to Yourself at First

It is hard to keep a secret

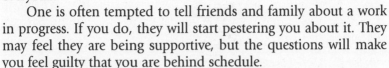

Early on, do not show your manuscript to anyone. When it is nearly done, show it to everyone.

One is often tempted to tell friends and family about a work in progress. If you do, they will start pestering you about it. They may feel they are being supportive, but the questions will make you feel guilty that you are behind schedule.

Cynthia Miller's manuscript was nearly complete. She had worked for years to compile the details on her collectibles. Finally, she announced to her colleagues that she needed just a few more items and her book would be done.

She received a quick reply from a distant acquaintance: "Don't write it; my book on collectibles is at the printer."

Of course, the competitor's book was not at the printer. The acquaintance was disappointed in his own lack of motivation and had not even touched the keyboard yet.

Do not waste time talking about what you plan to do. Spend the time doing it.

Never talk about what you are going to do until after you have written it.
—**Mario Puzo, author, *The Godfather*.**

Check Your Facts

Do not just copy resources out of other books.

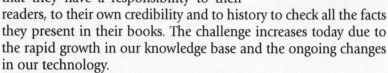

Nonfiction writers have long realized that they have a responsibility to their readers, to their own credibility and to history to check all the facts they present in their books. The challenge increases today due to the rapid growth in our knowledge base and the ongoing changes in our technology.

When *The Self-Publishing Manual* was revised for the 11th time, editor Karen Stedman contacted each reference in the text and each supplier listed in the 34-page Resources section. She discovered that an astounding 85% of the addresses had changed since the last edition—in just 13 months!

Most changes were area codes but there were also changes to email addresses, web sites, fax numbers and even some street addresses.
http://www.ParaPublishing.com

Check all your facts, not just the addresses. When you write a book, you are *committing history.*

When you speak, your words echo only across the room or down the hall. But when you write, your words echo down the ages.
> —**Bud Gardner, co-author,** *Chicken Soup for the Writer's Soul.*

Hire a Copy Editor

The Fourth Draft is the copy edit; the cleanup.

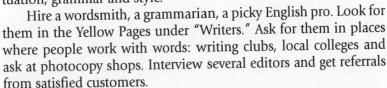

Now the manuscript is complete and you are concerned with punctuation, grammar and style.

Hire a wordsmith, a grammarian, a picky English pro. Look for them in the Yellow Pages under "Writers." Ask for them in places where people work with words: writing clubs, local colleges and ask at photocopy shops. Interview several editors and get referrals from satisfied customers.

The editor returned the manuscript and the pages were filled with red marks. Attached was an apologetic note saying, "I am sorry for the mess but I thought you would want to know about the errors." The author called the editor and thanked her. "I would much rather that you find the mistakes now than have my readers find them later."

According to Brenner Information Group, editors average 61 hours of work per book.

There is nothing wrong with unpolished writing, but there is no excuse for not having it cleaned up by an editor.

Editing is a *rewording activity*. Edit, edit, edit.

There is no such thing as a publishable first draft.
—William Targ, bookseller, collector, editor and publisher.

Know When to Call a Book Doctor

The final manuscript is your responsibility.

It is the author's responsibility to deliver a well-written, ready-for-publication manuscript to the publisher. Editors at publishing houses are no longer responsible for making major changes. If the manuscript needs restructuring or rewriting, the solution is often an outside book doctor. Book doctors are to writing as emergency room surgeons are to medicine: the specialist to call when the patient needs extensive help fast.

National Press Books called in Dick Côté to rewrite Edward Lee Howard's *Safe House: The Compelling Memoirs of the Only CIA Spy to Seek Asylum in Russia.* Accused of spying for the Russians, Howard wrote his book to document his innocence. However, the manuscript arrived 14 months late and lacked key pieces of information. In addition, after speaking Russian for nine years, his English had deteriorated. The assignment: Fly to Moscow, interview Mr. Howard and his KGB protectors, ask him all the questions the CIA and FBI were dying to ask, come home, and rewrite the entire book from scratch, all within 27 days. It was delivered in 26.

If a manuscript is in critical condition—beyond first aid— don't contact an editor. Call a book doctor.

Hire a Proofreader

The more eyes, the better.

Do not try to proof your own work. You are too close to the manuscript and will miss some typographical errors. You need a professional with fresh eyes to proofread your work.

Your computer's spelling and grammar checkers are good for a first pass, but never rely on them exclusively.

Make sure your proofreader uses standard proofreading marks so the corrections will be clear to all. For a chart of proofreaders' marks, see your dictionary.

Mother Nature's Nursery Rhymes, a children's poetry book, was done. Bill Sheehan was hand-carrying the art to his printer in Hong Kong. During the long flight, he noticed that bees and their activity were mentioned in a poem on page 15, but there were no bees in the accompanying illustration. Upon landing, he called Itoko Maeno, the illustrator, back at Advocacy Press in Santa Barbara. She suggested copying a bee from a previous page, and that saved the day.

advpress@impulse.net

There is more to proofing than just punctuation and spelling. And, it is never too late to proofread—again.

Do not skimp on proofreading. It is far more expensive to take ink off paper than to put it on.

When you publish a book, it's the world's book. The world edits it.
—Philip Roth, in the *New York Times Book Review*.

Use Quotations

Relevant quotations confirm your advice.

Quotations make the text more interesting; your book seems more important; and these words from others confirm your suggestions.

Quotations may be sprinkled throughout your text or may be used at the bottom of the pages. Quotations are best used when they are placed nearby to reinforce your words.

Bonnie Williamson, author of *A First-Year Teacher's Guidebook*, places quotations, humorous notes, statistics and tips in what she calls "pullouts." Her books are 8½ x 11 but the text is in 4¼"-wide columns, leaving a large outside margin. Her pullouts, placed in the margin, are fun reading and break up the text.
Bonniew@pacbell.net

Notice how quotations are used throughout this book to confirm these tips.

Gather quotations as you research your book. There are many fine quotation books and it is easy to find what you want online. Simply look for "quotations" with some of the search engines.

By the way, the word is "quotation" not "quote," which refers to a price or the cost of a service.

Nothing gives an author so much pleasure as to find his works respectfully quoted by other learned authors.
—Benjamin Franklin (1706–1790), author, printer, scientist and statesman.

Use Anecdotes

*Your audience remembers
the stories.*

Professional speakers have
long known that their audiences not only love stories, but
the yarns also amplify their
message. In fact, days later, the
stories (and their points) may
be all audience members recall.

Stories are used to illustrate a point just as effectively in nonfiction books as in other forms of communication.

Dr. Tom Plaut starts off his asthma books with stories. After reading
a few of these testimonials, it is clear that Dr. Plaut can help manage your
child's asthma. *Children with Asthma: A Manual for Parents* has sold over
200,000 copies.
http://www.pedipress.com

Jesus spoke in parables; he used short fictitious stories to
illustrate a moral attitude or a religious principle.

One reason stories work effectively is because they go directly
to the brain and entertain. They do not require the mental processing of more formal nonfiction writing. Stories have *heart* and
ring true.

Collect illustrative stories as you are collecting facts, quotations and other information for your book.

*Put it before them briefly so they will read it, clearly so they
will appreciate it, picturesquely so they will remember it and,
above all, accurately so they will be guided by its light.*
    —Joseph Pulitzer (1847–1911), American journalist.

Use Humor

Humor, like a story, makes your point and makes it memorable.

Occasional humor can make your writing more fun to read, but humor is one of the most difficult writing forms to master.

Harold Stephens made a jeep trip across Russia and ended up in jail; Milt Machlin, editor of *Argosy* magazine, wanted the story. When Machlin rejected the submission as "too heavy," Stephens explained that the experience "wasn't much fun."

Machlin said, "Tell me about it." Stephens described the arrest. He was told to strip down to his drawers. A woman interpreter was present when they told him to take off the underwear too. Stephens objected and she said, "Never mind, I'm married."

Machlin smiled and said, "Write it up." Stephens learned to laugh at himself and Machlin bought a dozen articles from him after that. Now Stephens uses humor in his books.

http://www.northcoast.com/~wolfen

Humor has two basic parts, the set-up and the punch line. In a book, your text is the set-up. All you have to do is see the humor in it. Humor is more effective when the punch line is a complete surprise; try to catch your reader off guard.

Your readers may even think you are a fun person.

Humor is the secret weapon of the nonfiction writer. It is secret because so few writers realize that it is often their best tool—and sometimes their only tool—for making an important point.
—William K. Zinsser, author, *On Writing Well.*

Add Illustrations

Say it with pictures.

Photographs, drawings, graphs, maps and charts illustrate, amplify and explain your words. People are more likely to buy your book if you stimulate their minds with both words and pictures.

It is the author's responsibility to come up with illustrations. Gather them as you write or have them drawn by an artist when you finish the manuscript. Have the same artist draw all the pictures to provide continuity.

Some publishers will reduce the number of illustrations to save money on production. Printing color photos is expensive because of the cost of color separations, coated paper and additional press time. On the other hand, black and white photos can be screened and dropped into the text for less than $10 each. The printer will not charge extra for line drawings.

Roy Maloney put over 400 photographs In *Real Estate Quick & Easy*. He credits the illustrations as the main reason the book has gone through 17 printings.
http://www.DropZonePress.com

Do not skimp on illustrations.

One picture, is worth a thousand words.
—Fred R. Barnard.

Combine Writing with . . .

Do two things at once.

One way to find time to write is to combine projects—to write while you are doing something else.

You might dictate on your daily walk, use your laptop when commuting on public transportation, or just think about your title and subtitle in the shower.

Dianna Booher has mastered the "interstate book": she has written a couple of books while driving. For example, she dictated the first draft of the 172-page *Clean up Your Act* (Warner) driving from city to city in Florida. Typically, she plans her book with *idea wheels* (in sequence and subordination) and then dictates from her outline. When she returns home, an assistant transcribes the dictation and Dianna begins the editing process—which may take three times as long.

http://www.BooherConsultants.com

Writing is best combined with projects that do not require concentration or thought. It is safer taking the train.

Lost time is never found again.
> **—Benjamin Franklin (1706–1790), author, printer, scientist and statesman.**

Get a Computer
You need the best tools.

The computer has become a writer's most important tool. It provides access to the Web for research, it helps writers draft their book faster, it makes editing easier, and it stores keystrokes to eliminate retyping.

Joe Sugarman says: "The computer has freed me to better emotionally express myself without fear of making a mistake or needing somebody else to assist in the retyping process.

"I can let myself go in the first draft knowing it is not perfect and feel secure that nobody will have to retype it. And, I can edit as often as I like. The computer was designed for editing."

Older writers who finally get a computer are usually delighted to find it unleashes their creativity and power.

Your computer does not have to be the most powerful available; word processing is basically all you really need.

Mechanics and carpenters know the value of having good tools; writers need the best equipment too.

Your computer should become transparent to your writing process. While it is only a tool, it happens to be the best writing tool ever developed.

> *Skeptics used to greet pioneering motorists with the cry 'Get a horse.' People who dismiss the impact of the personal computer, including many of the folks who use the machine, tend to employ the phrase 'It's just a tool.'*
> **—Peter Nulty.**

Choose to Type or Speak

*You'll wonder where the
yellow (pad) went.*

Speech-recognition software will speed the hardest part of writing your nonfiction book—the first draft. Now you can get the bulk of your materials onto the hard disk with your voice. Use an outline and speak into the microphone, giving punctuation and formatting commands as you go.

Dan Newman, a high school computer teacher, suffered repetitive-stress injuries from typing. He tried early speech-recognition systems and learned enough to become a consultant. Next he started a company and wrote guides to help his clients. To reach even more people, he used speech-recognition software to write two books on speech recognition: *The Dragon Naturally Speaking Guide* and *Look Ma—No Hands!* More books are on the way.
http://www.pcvoice.com http://www.SayICan.com

While speech-recognition software used to be very expensive, today it does not cost much more than a fancy keyboard. It will greatly speed your work—especially if you are not a rapid, accurate typist.

The three major suppliers of speech-recognition software are:

- Dragon Systems, http://www.dragonsys.com,
- IBM, http://www.ibm.com/viavoice, and
- Lernout and Hauspie, http://www.lhs.com

Today, talking to your computer will be a sign of intelligence, not insanity.
**—Headline in an ad for IBM's ViaVoice,
speech-recognition software.**

Practice Your Craft

Invest in personal development.

Nonfiction writers must know their subject and must know the craft of writing. Top athletes have coaches, and top musicians spend hours practicing. Writing, like any other skill, improves with practice.

Tro Harper, famous San Francisco book dealer, writes, "When I was a radio scriptwriter, I had a boss who gave me the best advice I ever got from anyone: professor, teacher, critic, or paid 'evaluator.' Bruce Chapman was a New York radio producer with a half dozen shows a week.

"One morning I handed him a script. He looked at it, then threw the first three pages in the wastebasket. He told me to practice by writing it again.

"Bruce didn't see himself as a teacher, but he made me write about what human beings do and say. He didn't want to know about deep thoughts. He wanted to know how people felt, what they did. Above all he wanted to be interested from the opening line, and entertained until the word *finis* appeared. 'OK, the roof fell in, the river is rising, the firemen are on their way, the police are banging on the door, the daughter is screaming. Tell me about it.' He made me practice. I never sit at my keyboard without remembering him."

TroHarp@PacBell.net

Practice makes perfect—or at least makes writing more salable. Take writing classes and write, write, write.

> *Just as a world-class athlete must practice no matter how much natural skill he or she may possess, a writer must practice, too.*
> **—Joe Sugarman, BluBlocker Corporation.**

Practice by Writing Short Stories

Small projects may not be easier, but they take less time.

One of the easiest ways to publication as well as to achieve recognition as a writer is to submit short true stories to the *Chicken Soup* books. Check the *Chicken Soup* web site for submission instructions. http://www.ChickenSoup. com. Buy a couple of *Chicken Soup* books and see the types of stories they are looking for.

Delve into your memory and tell your story. Make it sound like other *Chicken Soup* stories. Write and rewrite until it is irresistible—this is good practice.

Dan Clark is a short-story teller. He submitted some stories for the first volume of *Chicken Soup for the Soul* and three were chosen. Encouraged, he sent more. Since then, 30 of his stories have appeared in *Chicken Soup* books and 2 were in the Chicken Soup TV special.

His new book, *Puppies for Sale & Other Inspirational Tales*, was published by Health Communications, the *Chicken Soup* publisher, and made into a six-minute TV short starring Jack Lemmon. Dan subsequently co-authored *Chicken Soup for the College Soul*.

His submissions to *Chicken Soup* brought his work to the public. Now he has a publisher, ten books to his credit, and he made 255 speeches last year. http://www.ClarkSuccessSystems.com

To get a daily dose of *Chicken Soup*, subscribe to their listserv. To sign up, log on to http://SoupServer.com

They even pay $300 for stories used—and millions will read you. Hone your writing style by writing short pieces.

No horse has ever won a race it didn't enter.
—Anonymous.

Set Deadlines

Limits can help or hurt.

Many writers find deadlines stimulating. They just can't seem to concentrate until the writing is forced to the top of their to-do list.

"Okay, literary toilers, while some writers work at clean desks, plan ahead and easily meet their deadlines, most of us tend to fool around, stare at ceilings or out of windows until that date on the calendar looms large and threatening. IT'S DEADLINE TIME!

"Unscientific research among my colleagues leads me to believe that panic triggers creativity. Chemicals activate the brain and ideas and words begin to flow. If this is how it works for you, don't try to change things. Just allow enough time to rewrite and polish before submitting the manuscript.

"Finally, there are two major reasons to meet deadlines.

- Ego: we can't fail the editor or ourselves.
- Money: deliver the words, and eventually the check arrives."

—Frances Halpern, journalist and broadcaster.
fjsaga@compuserve.com

If it were not for the deadline of preparing for trade shows, industry would never get new products to market. Do not fight deadlines; embrace and meet them.

A deadline is negative inspiration. Still, it's better than no inspiration at all.
—Rita Mae Brown, writer and social activist.

When to Stop Writing

Once a writer, always a writer.

Write and rewrite until your manuscript is written as best as you can. However, there is no need to be a perfectionist where content is concerned.

You are finished writing when the manuscript is 98% *complete*—as long as it is 100% *accurate*. Waiting for one more photo or one more item of information is procrastination. It is time to give birth.

Hopefully, the first printing will sell out in three or four months, allowing you to update the book and go back to press. And you still will be only 98% complete because our society, science and industries are evolving so rapidly.

Larger publishers rarely keep a book alive past the first edition; they will reprint but they won't revise. On the other hand, many smaller publishers revise at each printing.

Your book is never finished. Parts of it become out of date the moment the ink strikes the paper. Your book is always a *work in progress*.

I'm never finished. Even once a book is published, I keep files for the next update.
—**Shel Horowitz, author, *Marketing Without Megabucks*.**

Encourage Reader Feedback

Listen to your readers.

Writing your book is not the end of your involvement. When readers have questions, authors have a responsibility to respond by email, mail, telephone and in person at book signings and other events.

Use these opportunities to gather material for the book's revision or your next book. Maybe you were not clear enough in your writing or perhaps the customer is interested in an important area you did not cover.

Bernard (Bear) Kamoroff, CPA, displays at book fairs and other industry events for the express purpose of gathering user feedback for *Small Time Operator* (23 revised editions and 53 printings in 21 years). At one fair, a woman said the business book was not for her because she was self-employed. So, Kamoroff added to the cover: "For All Small Businesses, Self-Employed Individuals, Employers, Professionals, Independent Contractors, and Home-Based Businesses." Also, due to customer feedback, he has increased the index from three pages to seven.
Tel: 800-515-8050

If people are asking questions, they like your work. Note their questions and your responses in a "correction copy" of your most recent edition and keep it on your shelf so you will be able to easily find the updates when the inventory runs low. Put the new information in your next revised edition—and sell it to them again.

Your best customer is one you have sold to previously.

I listen more and talk less. You can't learn anything when you're talking.
—Bing Crosby (1904–1977), American singer and film actor.

"Sometimes I turn ink into magic.
Other times, I just murder trees."
—**Randall Williams, Black Belt Press.**

Chapter Two
Why Write?

There are many justifications for investing your time and money in writing a nonfiction book. Some are fame, fortune, to help other people and/or because you have a personal mission.

Few things can boost a company's image like a book. Look at what Lee Iacocca's books did for Chrysler, John Sculley's book did for Apple, and Harvey Mackay's books have done for his envelope company. Marriott, Hilton, Volkswagen and many politicians have books. They know a book will advance a cause, give them more credibility, bring in more business and/or provide a new profit center.

Would you like to be recognized as someone who knows what he or she is talking about? Be someone worth listening to? Would you like to get paid for what you know? Would you like a job that is stimulating, interesting and challenging, a job you look forward to? Wouldn't it be nice to do what you love and love what you do?

Invest your time in your future. The foundation for the rest of your life is your book.

There are three reasons for becoming a writer: the first is that you need the money; the second, that you have something to say that you think the world should know; the third is that you can't think what to do with the long winter evenings.
—Quentin Crisp, author, How to Have a Lifestyle.

Cherish Fame

Authors are held in high esteem by our society.

Imagine people coming up to you at a business meeting or industry convention with a copy of your book and requesting an autograph. Imagine passing a bookstore and seeing your book in the window. Imagine being interviewed for a magazine article.

Actor Cynthia Hunter returned to her high school reunion in Minnesota. Classmates were impressed that she had gone to Hollywood and had appeared in numerous films and TV shows. When she slipped out to do a radio interview, the word quickly spread among her classmates that she had written a book to help actors break into the business and was chatting live on the biggest AM station in town.

By the next evening, *author* Cynthia Hunter had achieved celebrity status with her classmates. They bragged they knew the author of a brand new book: *Hollywood, Here I Come!* Being an author was even more important than being an actor.

Sports stars, movie stars and book authors achieve fame, but authors are also respected and revered for their knowledge.

Books through the ages have earned humanity's high regard as semi-sacred objects.
—Richard Kluger, author and editor.

Prepare for the Fans

Many fans want to mingle with you; they enjoy meeting a celebrity.

Your readers have invested their money in your book and have spent hours reading your words. They know much more about you than you know about them. They feel a connection and they often want to touch base with you.

Bob Johnson co-authored (with Patricia Bragg) the first book on the Triathlon in 1985. Soon after publication, he went to Hawaii to practice for the Ironman Competition. Being an active triathlete at 62 years of age gave him a great sense of pride, and his book launched him into notoriety.

He soon found himself surrounded by young groupies. While he tried his best to practice his running, biking and swimming privately, he was constantly followed.

http://www.bragg.com

Some of these fan encounters may even approach stalking but you must spend time with them. You would not be where you are without the fans.

A celebrity is a person who works hard all his life to become known, then wears dark glasses to avoid being recognized.
—Fred Allen (1894–1956), American comedian.

Be Careful of Pen Names

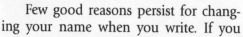

Pen names seem to be a major preoccupation with new writers.

Few good reasons persist for changing your name when you write. If you write porno books or write in two completely separate genres, or if you do not want your boss to know you are moonlighting or you wish to conceal your sex (readers seem to prefer female names on romance novels), you might have a reason.

Pseudonyms spread you too thin and confuse your readers. As you write, you will establish a following. Using more than one nom de plume means establishing a readership for each.

My brother Jim Poynter works in film; he selects locations and secures props. Early in his career, he thought it amusing to refer to himself as "Pat Pending." Soon he had business cards, letterhead and even credit cards in his stage name.

Later he was nominated for an Academy Award for his work on *The Right Stuff*. He attended the ceremony as Pat Pending and realized that old college classmates and other earlier acquaintances would not recognize his face or name.

You can't hide anyway. Your pen name will be listed in *Hawk's Authors' Pseudonyms*. Hawk@koyote.com

You are investing a lot of valuable time in your book. Are you sure you do not want credit for it? Unlisting your telephone number may be a necessity. Unlisting your name is not.

On the other hand, if your last book failed to sell well, changing your name could give you a fresh start in the industry.

Chance is perhaps the pseudonym of God when he does not wish to sign his work.
—Anatole France (1844–1924), French novelist and Nobel laureate.

Capitalize on Your Credibility

Your books are your credentials.

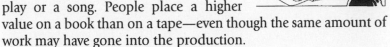

Writing a book provides you with more credibility than anything else you can do—more credibility than an audiotape, videotape, CD, a seminar, a screenplay or a song. People place a higher value on a book than on a tape—even though the same amount of work may have gone into the production.

Evel Knievel, the famous daredevil, aging celebrity and full-time madman, called Joe Vitale, wanting Joe to help him write his life story. Why did he call Joe? Because Joe wrote a book on P.T. Barnum, and Evel fancies himself a Barnum. While there are many writers out there, and many who have hounded Evel over the years, the daredevil went to Joe because of his other books, and because of one of his books in particular.

http://www.MrFire.com

Your books give you credibility and are the foundation for your other business.

For a person who has never led an army into battle, been elected to higher office, acted in movies or committed a heinous crime, a good book is the way to bridge the credibility gap.
—Rick Butts, author and speaker.

Beware of the Hazards

People will treat you differently.

Your life changes once you become a published author. Your status changes from that of a private person, the writer, to a public person, the author. The public becomes interested in you.

Your friends may also treat you differently once you have published a book. Some will be happy for you and supportive while others will be envious because they didn't write the book.

Gary Glenn was a fire investigator in Huntington Beach, California. With his wife, Peggy, he wrote a family fire safety guide titled *Don't Get Burned*.

The new firefighters treated Gary with awe, while some of the old-timers around the firehouse felt threatened or were jealous.

http://www.firebooks.com

Some authors thrive on notoriety while others are reclusive and uncomfortable with it. If you treasure your privacy, your book may become a love-hate object.

The nice thing about being a celebrity is that when you bore people, they think it's their fault.
—Henry Kissinger, statesman and Nobel laureate.

Value Your Authority

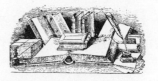

Your book makes you an authority on its subject matter.

You do not have to be an expert to write a book. When you write the book, you *become* the expert.

Gloria Wolk, MSW, researched viatical settlements to help her patients and then she wrote *Cash for the Final Days*, the first book on the subject. Next, she wrote a viatical investor's guide.

Investors began calling for advice on the risks of buying the life insurance policies of terminally ill people. Suddenly lawyers were flying in to consult with her. Realizing her new value, she raised her consulting rates to more than $200/hour. And they kept on coming.

Imagine the thrill when Jane Bryant Quinn's column on viatical settlements took up a full page in *Newsweek* and mentioned the title of Gloria's book, its price and her toll-free number.

Gloria is not a lawyer and yet she advises attorneys, judges and juries as an expert witness. Her books give her the credibility to be hired and the credibility to be believed.

http://www.viatical-expert.net

Once your book is published and you become an authority, your value and opportunities increase. You can charge more for seminars, articles, speeches and consulting.

> *The word* Authority *has the word* Author *in it.*
> –Joe "Mr. Fire" Vitale, author, *There's a Customer Born Every Minute*, a book on the life of P.T. Barnum.

Leave a Legacy

Your book is your gift to the world and it will last forever.

Evelyn Haertig spent 12 years on an expensive, full-color definitive treatise titled *Antique Combs & Purses*. A retired high school teacher and antiques dealer, she discovered there were no authoritative works on the subjects. She and her photographer husband examined museum collections around the world. Now she and her books are world authorities on the subjects.

Next, she sold her antique comb collection to publish *More Beautiful Purses*. When asked why she gave up her collection, Evelyn replied, "At my age, who needs a collection of combs? This book is more important; this book is my legacy."

Another example is Joe Vitale, who helps people write books. But books are not his most important product; he is really in the business of giving immortality.

You will live but a lifetime; your book will live forever.

> *A book is the only immortality.*
> **—Rufus Choate (1799–1859), American lawyer and senator.**

Amass Your Fortune

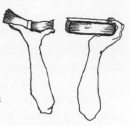

Write for the money.

Your book will be a new profit center. Approached properly, there is money in writing books.

It was a long flight home from the Maui Writer's Conference and the man in the seat next to me struck up a conversation. He finally got around to asking, "And what do you do?" I puffed up my chest proudly and announced, "I'm a writer."

"No, no," he quickly replied, "I mean, what do you do for a *living?*"
http://www.ParaPublishing.com

There are some starving writers out there but many of them are working on fiction, entertainment that is more difficult to sell. If you write nonfiction, put it in book form and publish the books yourself, you can do well financially.

Many authors work on their own schedule, give the world a piece of their mind and get paid (nicely) for it.

Write out of love, write out of instinct, write out of reason . . . But always for money.
**—Louis Untermeyer, poet, in *The New York Times*,
September 30, 1975.**

Advance Your Mission

A book enables you to get out the word on something you feel strongly about.

Donna Rae discovered the Scandinavian personal-care practice of *body brushing*. For beautiful skin, she dry brushes her body and follows with a quick shower rinse. Over the years, she spread the word far and wide through seminars, speeches and classes.

Then a Web search revealed there has never been a book on the subject. Encouraged, she conducted more research, sat down and wrote the book. She is reaching a lot more people—and the book (and product) have become a business.

http://www.BodyShine.com

When you have a sense of personal mission, your passion center becomes your profit center. Why split your energies? Take a stand. Be passionate. Do not be afraid to stir up controversy. Imagine sharing your enthusiasm with the rest of the world.

Certain books have exerted a profound influence on history, culture, civilization and scientific thought throughout recorded time.
  —Robert B. Downs, author, *Books That Changed the World*.

Inspire Others

You can help many other people with a how-to book.

Your experience and research may inspire a lot of people.

Darcie Sanders and Martha M. Bullen were publishing professionals who wanted to stay home with their children. They looked for books on going from the workplace to the homebase but found that few existed. With research and interviews, they wrote the book they needed. Little, Brown and Company published *Staying Home* through five printings; now the authors publish it themselves. http://www.spencerandwaters.com

Imagine the satisfaction you will feel in helping so many other people by sharing what you know.

With a book, you can make both a living and a difference.
—Michael Larsen, literary agent.

Realize You Know Something

Who am I to write this book?

We are so close to our subject that we often assume everyone knows what we know and everyone has our abilities and talent.

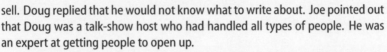

Doug Johnson is a well-known media person with one of the most popular radio shows in Texas. Joe Vitale was excited about being invited to the show. Joe found the show to be fun, but the off-air discussion was even more interesting.

Doug had written a novel, but Joe suggested he work on nonfiction because it is so much easier to sell. Doug replied that he would not know what to write about. Joe pointed out that Doug was a talk-show host who had handled all types of people. He was an expert at getting people to open up.

Joe suggested a book on how to have successful conversations, how to interview or how to talk in any situation. Doug responded with stories. Joe said, "Great, you can use them to illustrate your points."

Here was a famous celebrity talk-show host and it never occurred to him that he had a special talent or knew something unique.

http://www.MrFire.com

Who are you to write this book? The one who did the research and checked every detail.

Trust yourself. You know more than you think you do.
    —**Benjamin Spock, MD, author,** *Dr. Spock's Baby and Child Care.*

Chapter Three
Why a Book?

A nonfiction book is a product, an information product that is inexpensive to manufacture and easy to distribute. It is easy to protect with a $30 copyright registration.

A book speaks with more authority than other media.

When Bill Gates announced he wanted to publish a definitive 300-page discussion of his views on the information revolution, he made his proposal to book publishers. He did not elect to publish on-line, on CD-ROM or by fax. Bill Gates recognizes the book must come first.

One man is as good as another until he has written a book.
—Benjamin Jowett (1817–1893), British educator and Greek scholar.

Sell Products, Not Hours

Hours are few, products are many.

Most people sell their *hours*. Whether they work for someone else and punch a clock or are self-employed, they are selling their time. Some people charge more for their hours than others do. Doctors, for example, charge a great deal for their time.

The challenge is that even doctors have only 8, 10 or 12 hours a day to sell. Once those hours are sold, they stop earning.

A *product*, on the other hand, can keep on selling. Once you have developed it, it can sell even while you are sleeping. The ideal mix is to sell some of your hours and a lot of product.

Brian Tracy is a well-known, dynamic professional speaker who commands more than $10,000 per presentation. But his speeches also require a great deal of customizing and preparation time and lots of distant travel. His aim is to increase his inventory of books, tapes and other information/motivation products to achieve a 95% to 5% product-to-speaking mix. And, he is moving toward that goal.

http://www.BrianTracy.com

A book is a product; an ideal product.

I must govern the clock, not be governed by it.
—Golda Meir (1898–1978), Israeli prime minister and a founder of the state of Israel.

Realize the Value of Information

Information about a product or service earns more than the product or service itself.

Pick just about any product, service or industry and you will find that the consultants, seminar leaders and authors are making more money than the business owners.

Patti attended a real estate seminar to learn more about the speaker's angle on the business. Of course, the speaker was selling books and tapes in the back of the room (BOR sales).

Later she went to work for the speaker's seminar company and discovered the company made more money on books, tapes and seminars than on real estate.

She also discovered that she bought the wrong book. She did not need a book on real estate. She needed a book on how to write a book because there is more money in information.

Your nonfiction book contains valuable information that people will buy to save time and money.

The new source of power is not money in the hands of the few but information in the hands of many.
—John Naisbitt, author, *Megatrends 2000*.

Multiply Your Work

Spread your knowledge wisely.

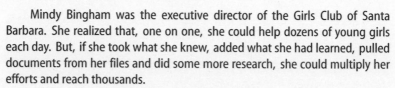

You can teach no more than a roomful of people at a seminar. You can help only a small group with private consulting. But your book multiplies your efforts and allows you to reach thousands, even millions.

Mindy Bingham was the executive director of the Girls Club of Santa Barbara. She realized that, one on one, she could help dozens of young girls each day. But, if she took what she knew, added what she had learned, pulled documents from her files and did some more research, she could multiply her efforts and reach thousands.

Choices, a Teen Woman's Journal for Self-Awareness and Personal Planning sold over a million copies so far and started a publishing company.

http://www.academicinnovations.com

Your book will affect more people than an audiotape, seminar or speech. Books are an efficient way to convey information to many people.

The most technologically efficient machine that man has ever invented is the book.
—Northrop Frye, Canadian author and educator.

Avoid Competition

Competitors will spar on price.

Make sure you have control over the product you wish to sell. Do not invest time and money producing and promoting a product that interested buyers can buy from someone else (often for less).

Joe Cossman was the originator and promoter of the Ant Farm, Spud Gun, Shrunken Head, Fly Cake and numerous other products. He would find local or imported products, nail down the source with a contract exclusive, have the products manufactured and then promote them. Joe has said for years that if you are going to promote a product, you must be the sole source.
http://www.cossman.com

If you control the product, you control the price. If you are not the sole (original) source, others will compete with you on the basis of price and the prices will decrease. It has been reported that 26% of book customers shop on the basis of price.

A manuscript can be copyrighted for only $30, giving you a legal monopoly to publish and sell it in any form you wish: hardcover book, audiotape, foreign language, video, film, etc.

Books are a safe product; your copyright makes you the sole source.

Who controls the past controls the future. Who controls the present controls the past.
—George Orwell (1903–1950), English author of
***Animal Farm* and *1984*.**

"There are three difficulties in authorship: to write anything worth the publishing, to find an honest man to publish it, and to get sensible men to read it."

—**Charles Caleb Colton,** *Lacon*, **1825.**

Chapter Four
What to Write

First, decide whether to entertain or inform. In other words, decide between fiction and nonfiction. As you will discover, nonfiction is easier to sell.

Focus on who your intended audience is and what you plan to give them. You must write to a particular group of readers and you must give them something they want. Since almost 300 books are published each day, the narrower your niche, the better your chance of not having competition.

You must also be able to locate your reader, the majority of whom may not frequent bookstores.

Start with shorter pieces for magazines and newspapers. Progress to book-length manuscripts for children, women, travelers, cooks or historians. Your Work might be a biography, inspirational or self-help book. Follow your interests.

Sell your writing over and over to other publications in the same and other forms. Wring maximum value out of your writing efforts.

> *I will never again go to people under false pretenses even if it is to give them the Holy Bible. I will never again sell anything, even if I have to starve. I am going home now and I will sit down and really write about people.*
> **—Henry Miller (1891–1980), American writer.**

Write Your Nonfiction First

Nonfiction is easier to sell.

Fiction is an art that comes from emotion; nonfiction is a craft derived from information.

As entertainment, fiction has to compete for peoples' time with other books, taking in a movie or playing with the kids. Nonfiction, on the other hand, does not compete for readers' time, with any other book or any other activity. Each nonfiction book is unique.

Hal Zina Bennett has written two novels, four children's books and more than 25 nonfiction books including *Write From the Heart*. He is good at, and likes doing both, but says, "Fiction does not pay as well."
TenacityPR@aol.com

Most publishers will urge you to work on your nonfiction first and to save your fiction until you can afford it. Spend your time writing how-to's—valuable information that people buy in order to save time or money.

Fiction writers tend to be creative, interesting people who are fun at parties. But nonfiction writers drive better cars.

It is better to have a permanent income than to be fascinating.
—Oscar Wilde (1854–1900), Irish-born writer and wit.

Make Sure You Will Have Readers

If you build it, will they come?

Before you even start writing, consider *who* will buy your book and what you plan to give them. Who is your primary audience? Your secondary audience?

"But everyone should read my book," Cheryl said, with a misty look in her eyes. Dan Poynter replied, "I write skydiving books and I want everyone to jump out of an airplane. But let's be realistic—not everyone will go skydiving. Now *who* will buy your book?"
http://www.ParaPublishing.com

The nonfiction book has to contain information people want to know or they will not part with a $20 bill to get it.

What associations do your prospective readers join and how large are their memberships? What are the circulations of the magazines your potential customers read? How many show up for specific annual events? Quantify your potential audience. Are there enough probable customers for your book? Be realistic.

All writing should be to a specifically targeted group that you research until you know it intimately. Aim for your readers' personal hot spots, in a writing style and level they are comfortable with. Learn how the group feels, acts, and what your audience likes or dislikes. Then, craft your writing in style and content specifically to your readership.
—Markus Allen, the Direct Mail Guru.

Make Sure You Can Locate Your Reader

Where is your potential customer?

And your answer is not "I'll reach them in bookstores."

Go into a bookstore on any given day. How many of the customers do you suppose are interested in a scuba book? Not many. What is the profile of the bookstore browser? It is the "recreational reader," someone used to plunking down $24.95 for hardcover fiction. But check out a dive shop and how many customers are interested in a book on scuba? Now the thinking-gears are turning.

Your book must have buyers and you must be able to locate them. Where will you find a high concentration of customers?

What type of stores do your potential customers frequent? Ask yourself, "What magazines do they read, what associations do they join and what annual events do they attend. Where are they?"

You want your books to be sold in bookstores but you will sell many more nonfiction books in specialty shops, to associations, through magazines and to specialty catalogs. Bookstores are the frosting, not the cake.

Make sure there is an audience for your book. Then promote your books where there is a high concentration of your potential customers.

To have great poets, there must be great audiences too.
—Walt Whitman (1819–1892), American poet.

Be Nimble

Start immediately and write faster.

It is a sad fact of book publishing life that the first book on a subject gets the most attention. The second to be published may be better, but it will be difficult to place in stores that already have that subject covered.

Diane Pfeifer was cruising the aisles at the annual Memorial Day weekend BEA Book Fair. This year, she noted there were a lot of angel books and she began to think about her specialty: parody cookbooks: *Gone with the Grits; Stand by Your Pan: The Country Music Cookbook; Quick Bytes: The Computer Lover's Cookbook,* and more). She continued to visit booths but kept on planning her *Angel Cookbook*.

On the third day of aisle cruising, her heart sank when she came upon a booth announcing an angel cookbook. Then she looked closer. The sign said, "Coming in December." Diane returned home and got right to work. Her *Angel Cookbook* came off the press in September.

http://www.readersndex.com/imprint/000002z/imprint.html

Since it takes most publishers 18 months to turn a manuscript into a book, chances are high you will be first if you publish yourself.

> *There is no less wit nor less invention in applying rightly a thought one finds in a book, than being the first author of that thought.*
> **—Pierre Bayle, political scientist and author,**
> **Dictionnaire Historique et Critique.**

Write What You Know

Experience counts.

You must have expertise or experience to be a credible nonfiction author. *Expertise* means you have an advanced degree in the field. *Experience* means you have lived it. You do not need a Ph.D. if you have personal experience, dedication to do research, and a deep desire to spread the word. The most important question is: Have you been there?

His engineering firm told Bob Bly he would have to relocate from New York City to the headquarters in Wichita, Kansas. His fiancée did not want to leave Manhattan, so he resigned and started a new career as a self-employed industrial writer, producing brochures and data sheets for chemical companies and industrial equipment manufacturers.

The transition from employee to freelancer was an educational experience, one he knew many others would go through (or hope to some day). The experience became the topic of his book, *Out on Your Own: From Corporate to Self-Employment*, published by John Wiley and Sons.

http://www.bly.com

A fresh outlook can be an asset. When you are beginning in a new field, you have the same questions your readers will have. Write as you learn, record as you study and blossom as you grow. Then run your manuscript by other experts on your subject matter to make sure you have not left anything out or written something you misunderstood. That is your third draft and it is called peer review.

> *You must have experience to write a good nonfiction book, so please do not write a book on how to get rich unless you are already rich.*
> **—Patricia Clay, actress.**

Write What Interests You

What do you want to be doing in three years?

Plan your future and your book now. It is best not to write on something that you are no longer interested in and do not want to pursue.

For example, let's say you have been selling cars for the past ten years, but your hobby is golf and you are pretty good at the game. Do not write on cars even though you are an expert. Write on some aspect of golf. Once your book is published, people will request interviews, articles, seminars and consulting. Plan now to make sure they approach you on a subject you are passionate about.

Rich and Sue Freeman never intended to become writers. After 20-odd years climbing the corporate ladder, they requested six-month leaves to hike the Appalachian Trail from Georgia to Maine. Some 2,200 miles later, they conquered Mount Katahdin only to hear they would not be returning to the company. They had been downsized.

With all options open to them, they decided to share their newfound love of the outdoors. They kept hiking, researching, writing and applying their years of corporate knowledge to running the business.

Their first effort was a guidebook on the trails around their hometown that could be used by people of all ages out for a stroll. Books on hiking trails led to guides on biking trails and then to publishing other outdoor-recreation authors. Their income dropped the first year but they were alive with a new passion. The latest book from Footprint Press is *Bruce Trail: An Adventure Along the Niagara Escarpment*.

http://www.footprintpress.com

Do not write about what you *used* to do; pursue what you *want* to do.

> *My object in living is to unite my avocation and my vocation.*
> —**Robert Frost (1874–1963), American poet,**
> *Tramps in Mudtime.*

Write About Your Hobby

Write what you love and love what you write.

If you love your *work*, writing about some aspect of your industry will be fun and advance your position in your field.

If you write about your *hobby*, you will spend time studying an area you enjoy.

Participants write the best how-to books.

Doug Werner loves sports and the outdoors so much that he moved back to Southern California. When surfing became an obsession, he moved to San Diego. He soon saw a need for a beginner's book; he wrote and published *Surfing Start-Up* in 1993. Then a mission took shape: to learn about and write start-up books on other sports. He was in the perfect location: Southern California has the weather, terrain and the activities.

One by one, he tackled, learned, wrote and published start-up books on fencing, backpacking, bowling, boxing, sailing, longboard surfing, snow-boarding, inline skating and golfing. He is building his publishing company one book at a time.

Doug loves learning new sports and introducing readers to them. Writing allows him to earn a living in his hobbies.

http://StartUpSports.com

Write about what you like to do when you are not working and the writing won't seem like work.

The trouble with gardening is that it does not remain an avocation. It becomes an obsession.
> —**Phyllis McGinley, author,** *The Province of the Heart,*
> **1959.**

Write Your Family History

Publish your roots.

Nearly everyone is interested in Number One, himself or herself, and, therefore, who he or she is and where he or she came from. People want to know more about their family and their roots.

Today, the computer and the Web make it easier than ever to compile and distribute heraldic information.

Pro CD, for example, can provide you with all the addresses and telephone numbers on CD. It is easy to print out a list of people with your family name. Web sites such as http://aprilfools.infospace.com/lookup_e.htm will help you find email addresses.

Contact people with your surname for family trees, history and photographs.

Start with a newsletter and distribute it via inexpensive email. Use the newsletter to request more information. Grow your information base and build your mailing list.

Then after a couple of years, pour all your family material into a book and sell it to your relatives, libraries and the public. Be sure to produce a limited number of more expensive leather-bound editions.

See the genealogy sites at http://www.ngsgenealogy.org and http://cyndislist.com

The bond that links your true family is not one of blood, but of respect and joy in each other's life. Rarely do members of one family grow up under the same roof.
—Richard Bach, author, *Jonathan Livingston Seagull*.

Write for Children

It takes one to know one.

Some beginning writers think writing for children will be easier than writing for adults. Children are pretty sharp, and their attention span is usually much shorter.

Allana Elovson, a self-publisher of books about parenting, was reading to a young niece one day. The story was well received: The child was fascinated by all the pictures and listened intently.

When they finished the book, she smiled at her aunt and knowingly explained that the words were there for people who cannot read pictures.

Women buy 82% of all children's books and half are bought as gifts. Nearly 40% of the books are bought by mothers. Hardcover children's books are currently selling for an average of $14.51, while softcovers are going for $7.34. Hardcovers with a dust jacket go for more than books without jackets.

According to *Publishers Weekly*, children's books fall into the following categories: 27% picture books, 17% books for babies and toddlers, 20% for younger readers, 19% for middle readers, and 17% for young-adult readers. Decide which category your work falls into.

Generally speaking, children's books are considered 50% text and 50% illustration, so royalties are split between the writer and the illustrator. If the royalty is 10%, then the writer and the illustrator each get 5%.

Children's books tend to have a longer life than adult books. They start off slow and build over time. According to *USA Today*, October marks the beginning of a steady climb in the sales of children's books toward the holidays.

Be upbeat and send a positive message. So often children's stories center around mistakes and punishment, which sends a subtle message to a child about not taking risks for fear of harm.

The secret to writing a successful children's book is not to think like a child or to try to remember what it was like to be a child, but to still be a child within.
    —Andrea Brown, literary agent.

Write to Women

Give your customer what she wants and needs.

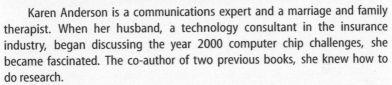

Women purchase 68% of all trade books. If you aim your message at women, a great majority of the potential buyers will *identify* with your book. For example, it only took *Chicken Soup for the Woman's Soul* six months to sell as many copies as the original *Chicken Soup for the Soul* sold in its first three years.

Karen Anderson is a communications expert and a marriage and family therapist. When her husband, a technology consultant in the insurance industry, began discussing the year 2000 computer chip challenges, she became fascinated. The co-author of two previous books, she knew how to do research.

The more research she did on Y2K, the more concerned she became. When it was time to go to press, she still had not decided on a title.

Then she discovered that women purchase most books. She re-slanted the text and titled the book *Y2K for Women: How to Protect Your Home and Family in the Coming Crisis*. She printed 10,000 copies and then sold the rights to Thomas Nelson Publishers.

http://www.y2kwomen.com

Women will listen to women talking about women's issues.

The great question that I have not been able to answer, despite my 30 years of research into the feminine soul, is 'What does a woman want?'
> —Sigmund Freud (1856–1939), Austrian physician and founder of psychoanalysis, in the *Atlantic Monthly*.

Write a Cookbook
Everyone eats.

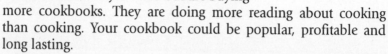

Even though thousands of cookbooks are published each year, they have an impressive history as best sellers.

Many people are cooking less but obsessing about it more. They are eating out more than they used to but are buying more cookbooks. They are doing more reading about cooking than cooking. Your cookbook could be popular, profitable and long lasting.

Back in 1933, Harriet Ross Colquitt collected recipes (she called them "receipts") from some of the outstanding black cooks around Savannah, Georgia. Next, she added recipes for traditional dishes from her own family. Then she updated the language and filled in interesting background on the recipes. The food customs of the region were rescued with the publication of *The Savannah Cookbook: A Collection of Old Fashioned Receipts from Colonial Kitchens*.

Many cookbook buyers now are also interested in books with personal stories behind them written by people who have something inspiring to tell or some interesting information to relate.

Some cookbook authors use *Micro Cookbook 5.0* to catalog and organize their recipes.

http://www.imsisoft.com/microCookbook

The biggest seller is cookbooks and the second is diet books—how not to eat what you've just learned how to cook.
—Andy Rooney, *And More by Andy Rooney.*
Sage commentator on *60 Minutes* **and three-time Emmy Award winner.**

Write a Travel Book

Travel and write about it.

The World Tourism Organization predicts that by 2020, travel will be the world's biggest industry. Travelers will need guidebooks.

Be prepared. Learn the history and become an expert on the area. Inject humor if you can. Travel publications are always looking for humor. Try to stand out from the crowd. Your story must have a personal voice and a point of view. Say something new about your subject. What is it about the place that impressed or depressed you? Avoid trite phrases and think of creative descriptions.

Author-publisher Gordon Burgett has written a lot of travel articles and books. Having spent considerable time in South America, he researched the area. He found that there was very little tourist information on Paraguay. So, just after the dictator Stroessner left the country, Burgett made a trip south to gather information for a book. Only then did he discover the lack of infrastructure and amenities—and the reason there is little tourist information on the country.

Be patient and persistent. If you find other writers going after the same story, adjust. And do your homework.

Of all possible subjects, travel is the most difficult for an artist, as it is the easiest for a journalist.
—**W.H. Auden, author, poet,** *The Dyer's Hand* **(1962).**

Write Anthologies

Anthologies are collections of writings from several people. They are compiled and arranged by an editor.

Some anthologies are a loose collection of essays on a single area or subject. They bring together several creative people (fiction) or several experts (nonfiction).

Some collections are published "as is," while in others the stories are rewritten by one person so that they sound a great deal alike.

Dottie Walters, publisher of *Sharing Ideas* magazine, has published 36 anthologies so far. Each book has a separate title and theme such as *Humor, Leadership, Marketing, Mentoring* and so on. Each contribution comes from a professional speaker.

She prints a different dust jacket for each contributor featuring his or her photo, name and biography. Each contributor has a customized book on his or her speaking topic and each orders and pays for a certain number of books before the project goes to press. The books not only give them more credibility, leading to more speaking business, but they now have a product to sell in the back of the room (BOR).

Dottie says: "The word 'anthology' literally means 'a bouquet of flowers.' We call our anthology books 'Bouquets of Ideas.'"

http://www.walters-intl.com

One of the earliest anthologies was the Bible. It has several authors including Matthew, Mark, Luke and John.

By some might be said of me that here I have but gathered a nosegay of strange flowers, and have put nothing of mine unto it but the thread to bind them.

—**Michel de Montaigne (1533–1592), French writer, in *Essays*.**

Write a Column
Find a need and fill it.

To write a column for a periodical, you must find a subject it does not cover and convince the editor that your writing will attract readers. Newspaper owners want to sell papers.

Frances Halpern visited the editor of a small community newspaper to ask if she could write a weekly column. The editor turned her down, saying he receives these offers all the time and what he needs are writers who will maintain quality and meet deadlines.

She went home and wrote three columns. Her cover letter assured him she would meet deadlines. After her column ran for a year, she was hired full-time. Later, she became a columnist for *The Los Angeles Times*.

fjsaga@compuserve.com

Many columnists have banked their columns and grouped them into books. The newspaper subscribers become primary customers.

Sell the words to your readers again in a different format.

A magazine or a newspaper is a shop. Each is an experiment and represents a new focus, a new ratio between commerce and intellect.
—John Jay Chapman, author, *Practical Agitation*, 1898.

Then Syndicate Your Column

After filling the initial need, find more needs and use the same fill.

Syndicates will distribute your column or cartoon to newspapers across the country. In exchange for 40-60% of the fee, they take care of the administration. Alternatively, you can self-syndicate.

Unless you are a well-known expert or celebrity, getting a column syndicated is a challenge. You must convince editors that your expertise, writing ability and fresh approach will make readers care and think.

Begin the process by studying your local newspapers and magazines. Write at least three sample columns and nag, cajole and charm an editor into taking a chance on you. After the column finds its first home and attracts a positive response, go after new markets. You now have published material and fan letters to intrigue more editors.

Columnist and talk-show host Frances Halpern tells of one woman with a passion for theater and the arts who came up with the idea of writing for senior citizens. Her column about entertainment, focusing on the interests of older people, is now syndicated to a number of senior newspapers.
fjsaga@compuserve.com

See the *Features Available* advertising section of *Editor & Publisher* magazine. http://www.MediaInfo.com

Multiply your efforts by publishing your work in several periodicals simultaneously.

> *I get up in the morning with an idea for a three-volume novel and by nightfall it's a paragraph in my column.*
> **—Don Marquis (1878–1937), American writer and columnist.**

Write for Trade Magazines

It is easier to re-slant and resell an existing article than to write a new one.

Many authors start off by writing for magazines. This non-fiction writing enables them to bank material for their book, improve their writing style and build up a loyal readership.

Savvy magazine writers sell the same article over and over by re-slanting it for the next magazine and the next. Some articles are even sold simultaneously, without being changed.

Author-publisher Gordon Burgett was driving home when he heard Paul Harvey tell a story about a lost cat that had found its way home over several hundred miles. The next day, he read of a goat that found its way home. The next week, he read about "psi-trailing," animals finding their way home even when their owners move. He began studying the phenomenon and wrote an article that he sold to one magazine. Since 1983, the article has been printed in different forms in 18 magazines and some 30 reprints (unchanged). Over the years, Gordon has sold over 1,800 articles. This one article amounts to 2% of them.

http://www.sops.com

Over 18,000 magazines are published in the United States according to the Magazine Publishers of America.

Trade magazine editors want new ideas; they don't require Pulitzer Prize winners.
—Mary Maurer, writer, in *The Portable Writers' Conference*.

Stay in One Field . . .

And own it.

Once you select your subject, stick to it; stay in one field. Too many authors write a book on a subject they know well—aimed at their own (reachable) field. With this formula, the book is a success, and they suddenly think selling books is easy, so they write about a totally different subject. It flops because they do not know how to reach the buyers in this particular market.

One day, I received a call from a customer. He said, "I'm a chiropractor, and I recognize that while chiropractors are good at what they do, they are not good at running their offices. But I have solved that challenge. I have just finished my book titled *How to Run Your Chiropractic Office.*"

"Sounds good," I said, and I thought to myself: "Now here is an author who can look into the mirror and see a reflection of his customer. He knows who the customer is, what the customer needs and (most importantly) where the customer is."

Then the doctor went on, "I have a packaging idea I would like to run by you." I leaned back in my chair and listened. The caller said, "Once I sell this book to all the chiropractors, I'll go through the manuscript with search & replace and change the word 'chiropractor' to 'dentist' and sell the same book to all the dentists. Next, I'll sell to all the medical doctors. Isn't that a great plan?"

"No," I said, "it sounds great but it's a terrible idea. First off, it will not be all that easy to sell your peers. It will take reviews in your magazines, displays at your conventions, lots of mail and telephone calls. Finally, word of mouth from one doctor to another will sell the book.

"Do you really want to learn all about dentists—read their magazines, join their associations and attend their conventions? You don't have time for that.

"What you should do is publish this book. Then do the advanced book, then the office forms book, and then the little books chiropractors give to their patients. You want to become known as the publisher for the chiropractic industry."

http://www.ParaPublishing.com

New customers have to be bought; existing customers are free. Anyone who has ever been in sales will tell us that it is far easier to sell an additional product to an existing customer than it is to find a new customer. Stay in one field and keep adding products until you own the field.

Next, combine your products in a "power pack," a higher priced package.

The average sale is made after the prospect has said 'no' six times.
—Jeffrey P. Davidson, author and speaker, in
The Washington Post, 1985.

Recycle Your Work

Sell subsidiary rights.

When you write a manuscript, you are creating a *Work*. The Work may be published in several different formats (editions): hardcover, softcover, audiotape, foreign languages, magazine condensation, newspaper serialization, movie, etc. These are called "subsidiary rights."

Dan Burrus sold and published six different rights to *Technotrends*. The hardcover rights went to HarperBusiness, the audio rights to Harper Audio, the softcover to HarperBusiness, the Technotrends Business Strategy Card Game to United States Games Systems, the video was published by Burrus Research and Burrus also published the *Technotrends* newsletter.
http://www.burrus.com http://www.burrus.com

Keep your rights separate. Publish some editions yourself and sell some to other publishers. Wring maximum value out of your Work.

The bottom line makes it abundantly clear; subsidiary rights have become less and less subsidiary.
—Nancy Evans, editor.

Record Your Book

You are more than an author, a publisher or a publicist; you are an information provider.

Nonfiction authors provide information and you should provide your information in any form your readers want: books, special reports, audiotapes, videotapes, speeches, seminars, consulting, etc.

Some of your customers want your guidance (information) but are too busy to read your book. Some may commute a long distance and want your help on tape. They have time to listen to you.

Once your book is out, use it as a script and record an audiotape album. Bundle the book with the tape set so those listeners can find the text they wish to review without searching the whole (linear) tape.

Viz-Ability marketing specialist Raleigh Pinskey sold *You Can Hype Anything* to Carol Publishing. Then she redrafted the text into the spoken word (with contractions), recorded it and self-published the tape album. Her next book, *101 Ways to Promote Yourself*, was sold to Avon and she sold the audio rights to B&B Audio.
http://www.PromoteYourself.com

You are selling your expertise and research—it is called *information*.

Spoken-word audio tapes turn your car into a university.
—Judit Sinclair, author, *Making Pigs Fly*.

Sell Foreign Language Rights

*Have your book read
around the world.*

By having your book translated
into other languages, more people
will benefit from your message.

English is the business language of the world, it is the aviation language, it is the Web language, it has replaced French as the diplomatic language and German as the scientific language. Worldwide, more people speak English as a second language than any other. But given a choice, many people would prefer to read your book in their first language.

Language rights are sold to publishers in other countries. They translate the book, design it, typeset it, have it printed and then plug it into their existing distribution system.

Christine Harvey was vacationing in France with her husband. She had written ahead to five publishers, giving them her dates in Paris, and suggesting appointment times. When she arrived at the first meeting, she spread her press clippings all over the assistant editor's desk, but wouldn't show him the book until he was convinced about her credibility.

Finally, in desperation he begged, "Please Mrs. Harvey, can I see the book?" He said he would show it to the editor-in-chief, and give her an answer in three weeks. "Oh no," Christine said, "I have to see him myself now because I'm leaving Paris Friday and need an answer by then. I'm showing the book to two other publishers."

He kept insisting that a meeting was impossible. Then the editor-in-chief walked in and saw all the clippings. While the assistant was still arguing with her, the boss handed her his card and whispered out of earshot of his assistant, "Call me on Friday."

Christine called and his answer was "YES." Since then, her books have been translated into 21 languages and published in 49 international editions.

ChristineHarvey@CompuServe.com

Contact the publishers' associations in Germany, France, Italy, Spain and Japan. See *International Literary Marketplace* or visit their exhibits at book fairs. Ask them to recommend publishers that specialize in your type of books.

Match your book to the international publisher; they are the ones to contact. They know what you are talking about and they know where to sell your book.

Babel; because the Lord did there confound the language of all the earth.
—Genesis, 11:9.

Retain Your Electronic Rights

Anticipate the future.

Electronic rights refers to any computer-related media. It is hard to predict the forms in which your book might be published ten years from now.

A few years ago, some of the big New York publishers were shocked to find they did not buy the electronic rights when they originally negotiated with their authors. Their lawyers did not anticipate CDs and the Web when they drafted the contracts. With the advent of CDs and the Web's need for content, electronic subsidiary rights suddenly had great potential value.

The publishers quickly added ebooks to their new contracts and tried to persuade their existing authors to sign over their electronic rights.

Make sure your contracts cover electronic rights and other forms of publication not yet invented. And reserve those rights to yourself.

If your publisher insists on retaining the electronic rights (to sell), give them the rights for 90 days. If they sell the rights quickly, you both win. If not, you are free to sell them yourself. Do not let your publisher tie up and sit on valuable rights.

The careful author and publisher will distinguish between several major categories of electronic rights, and they will be mindful of new categories that will emerge as new technologies develop.
—**Jonathan Kirsch, attorney, author,**
Kirsch's Guide to the Book Contract.

Chapter Five
Research

Most of a nonfiction writer's time is spent in study. You must locate and read through all the relevant materials available in other books, magazines, newsletters, newspapers, interviews, museums, historical societies, public libraries, university libraries and special (law, medical) libraries. You have an obligation to your audience, to your book and to yourself to exhaust every possible source of information.

Today, in addition to the above resources, you have access to the Web, the world's largest library. You must spend hours and hours searching for both information and potential customers. Also, check to see if you have any competition for this book.

Only you know how far back your research must go. If you are writing about parachutes, you will have to investigate back at least to 1495 and Leonardo da Vinci. If you are researching computers, three months may be far enough.

Whether you are writing fiction or nonfiction, you must check and verify every fact and resource. (You owe it to your reader, you owe it to your book and you owe it to yourself.)

History does not repeat itself. Nonfiction writers repeat each other.

The man is most original who can adapt from the greatest number of sources.
—Thomas Carlyle (1795–1881), Scottish essayist and historian.

Gather Information

How much material is available?

Before you set off on your writing journey, you must conduct some research. You want to know how much information is available on the subject, if this book has been done before and whether there is a market for it. Once you see what is out there, your approach, angle, hook, direction or niche may change. Research will provide material and help you quantify your project.

Sidney J. Smith, happily married for many years, was deeply troubled by the high rate of divorce. So, he developed a number of key questions that a couple contemplating marriage should ask each other. Then he realized he could reach more people if he put the questions into a book.

He visited a large bookstore and could find only one book like the one he contemplated, and it was rather dry and clinical.

A Web search found several sites on preparing for marriage, so he concluded that there are a lot of people interested in the subject. Encouraged, he charged ahead on *Before Saying Yes to Marriage: 101 Questions to Ask Yourself.*

Research has a stimulating effect. Your book will take shape in your mind as you figure where each new fact will fit in.

Never skimp on your research. So-called writer's block is invariably the result of too little research. If you know enough, you won't have trouble filling as many pages as you want to.
—Louise Purwin Zobel, author, The Travel Writer's Handbook.

Learn on the Writing Journey

We rarely know our destination until our arrival—when we complete the book.

Many writers begin with a proposal, a *business plan* for the book. They draft the back-cover sales copy and then a preliminary table of contents. Finally, they fill in the individual chapters.

But as these writers research other books, articles, journals and interview sources, they learn more about the subject. Often, they discover new information and the book takes off in a new direction.

Literary consultant and author Mary Embree had experience as a stop-smoking therapist. To reach more people with a book, she drafted a proposal and sent it to an agent. The agent turned down the proposal, saying there were too many books on the subject.

Mary continued her study and discovered a lot of medical research on women and smoking that had not been published. Apparently, women and men react differently to nicotine.

She rewrote the proposal and *A Woman's Way: The Stop-Smoking Book for Women* was sold to WRS Publishing. Later she spun off a smoking cessation workbook and a booklet based on the same material.

Mary is the founder of the Small Publishers, Artists and Writers Network (SPAWN).

http://www.spawn.org

Writing is a research journey. You learn when you write.

I write to find out.
—William Manchester, author, historian.

Get More Detail

Nonfiction books are written from research plus personal experience.

Check every book written on your subject. Then check the magazines. Interview experts and make a field trip. Get all the background you can.

Author-consultant Penny Paine wanted her children's book to be set in Ireland and her main character to be a pig. So she spent three days walking around Newport on the west coast of the Emerald Isle, taking photographs, interviewing the locals and pretending to be a pig.

Penny searched out family names, special locations and local sayings for authenticity. She wrote it all down as she walked her story. *Molly's Magic* was so detailed, accurate and fun that it won a Parent's Choice award.

http://www.PennyPaine.com

Check every resource and get first-hand experience.

The greatest part of a writer's time is spent in reading, in order to write; a man will turn over half a library to make one book.
—Samuel Johnson (1709–1784), English lexicographer, author, *Dictionary of the English Language*.

Research on the Web

The Web is the world's largest library.

Online bookstore databases such as Amazon.com list all the books that are currently available or "in print" as well as out-of-print books. Make a *subject* search and print out the results. Try several alternative words. For example, for a book on parenting, try "parenting," "parent," "mother," "father," etc.

To be thorough, make a similar search for *titles* beginning with the same key words. Try several online book databases.

Next, make a search on your proposed or *working* title. Make sure it has not been used recently. Then join listservs.

Cy Stapleton was trying to find enough material to fill four columns each month for several printing trade journals.

His solution was to set up an email listserv and offer free subscriptions to printers. The claimed purpose of the list was to give printers a forum to discuss problems and share ideas with each other. The "real" purpose was to give him ideas of what topics deserved a little ink. Both purposes have been served admirably.

The list now has almost 500 printers subscribed and he has a constant stream of new ideas. They also do his research. A 1,200-word column that used to take days to research and write can now be written in a couple of hours.

http://www.hotlinecy.com

See how much information is available on your subject. Gather details from every book, magazine article, database and resource. Visit the web sites listed in the appendix and use search engines.

This detective work can be great fun. One scrap of information will lead to another as you become lost in cyberspace.

Now you do not have to drive to the library; you can research your book from home.

On the Web, a journey of a thousand leagues begins with the first keystroke.
—Scott Gross, speaker, author, Positively Outrageous Service.

Learn from Experience

Writing your second book will go more smoothly.

Like any other project, the second time around is easier. Your second book will be less complicated to write, produce and promote.

The book writing and publishing business is relatively easy. It seems difficult because it is very different from other businesses. There are many details to learn. Your editorial, business and promotion research is an investment in future books.

If you have ideas for several books, put some space between them so that you may learn from each. Put 12 months between one and two, 9 months between two and three, 6 months between three and four and 3 months between four and five. By then you will know what you are doing. Each book has to be carefully written, properly produced and thoroughly promoted.

The greatest joy comes the day you get a call from a customer who wants your book. And you get to ask, "Which one?"

Blaze your trail on your first book and the second book will be much easier.

Experience is the best teacher.
   —Anonymous.

Get Reference Books

Look it up.

Even though your computer does a pretty fair job with spelling, grammar and the thesaurus, every writer needs some reference books. The computer is not infallible when it comes to language usage and it usually does not answer the question "Why?"

Jan Nathan, Executive Director of the Publishers Marketing Association, tells of an author/publisher who had his book professionally designed but decided to cut corners on proofreading. He relied on his computer's spell-checker.

After printing 5,000 copies, a colleague pointed out some misspelled words, both on the cover and inside. For example, the spell-checker did not catch the misspelling of "Foreword." All 5,000 covers announced the "Forward" by a very prominent person. By the way, this is a very common spelling mistake.

http://www.pma-onllne.org

The least expensive places to buy dictionaries, style manuals and other reference books are used book stores. See your local Yellow Pages. Some references, such as the Microsoft Bookshelf, are available on CD.

The best writers' thesauruses are dog-eared and worn with use.
—**Ardath Mayhar, author, in** *The Portable Writers' Conference.*

Attend Writers' Conferences

Get out of the house; network with your peers.

Writers' conferences are markets that bring buyers and sellers together. If you have a manuscript or an idea to pitch, conferences have the agents, editors and publishers you want to meet.

These events inform, entertain and console. They are a venue for being inspired by successful authors and a place to meet the (often) otherwise unapproachable editors, agents and publishers. You will also meet other writers who are trying to figure out the secret to getting published.

Author-speaker Leslie Charles attended the Maui Writers Conference to find an agent for her latest project. Patti Breitman liked her idea and Leslie liked Patti; they joined forces to smooth out the proposal. *Why Is Everyone So Cranky?* had three major bidders at auction, and while two tied, Leslie picked Hyperion and its six-figure advance.

LesChas@aol.com

Two of the larger, more successful and best-known annual events are the Santa Barbara Writers Conference in late June and the Maui Writers Conference over the Labor Day weekend.

Editors and agents troll for new talent at writer's conferences. Attend at least one a year and swim toward the bait.
—Paul Raymond Martin, author, The Writer's Little Instruction Book.

Chapter Six
Building Your Book

Make up a list of possible titles and subtitles. Then draft your back-cover sales copy.

Make your manuscript portable by placing it in a binder. And carry it around with you—always.

It is hard to put some time aside to write. But we all encounter unexpected bits of time throughout our day. They may be a few minutes after lunch, waiting in an office for an appointment or riding public transportation. Then you can get out the binder and work on your book.

With the binder under your arm, the project will be constantly active in your mind. As you visit a friend, walk on the beach or see a film, you will be searching for relevant ideas, stories, examples, quotations and sources.

Set up your binder with dividers for each chapter. Put a sketch of your cover on the front and your back-cover sales copy on the back. Insert your front matter pages: the title page, copyright page, table of contents, foreword, about the author, disclaimer and the rest.

Build the shell of your book and then begin to fill the sections.

The best time for planning a book is when you are doing the dishes.
—Agatha Christie, English mystery writer.

Get a Model Book

You do not have to reinvent the wheel.

What do you want your book to look like? Visualize. Visit a bookstore. Check the section where your book will be, then look into other sections. Find a book you like—on any subject. Consider the binding, layout, feel, margins, type style, everything. Then buy it.

Use this book as a *model*. Tell your editor, typesetter and printer you want your manuscript to look like this book.

Patricia went to a bookstore and noticed that the smaller mass-market paperbacks were fancier than other softcover books. The storeowner explained that the mass-market books were sold on newsstands and had to compete for attention with magazines.

She bought one she loved. The jacket had an embossed (raised) title and a hologram. She took it to her printer and said she wanted the same for the jacket of her hardcover book.

According to Brenner Information Group, graphic design consumes 13.5% of the budget for fiction titles and 3.7% of the budget for nonfiction titles.

Your typesetter and book printer can deliver any format you wish. Just give them some guidance.

There is no need to plan a book when you can adapt an existing great design.

Creativity should be admired but copying is faster.

Fashion Your Book Like the Others in Its Field

In book design, different doesn't sell.

As you survey the shelves in the bookstore, you will note that each genre or category has its own unique look. For example, business books usually have a hard cover and a dust jacket. Books for professionals such as doctors, lawyers and accountants are hardcover without a dust jacket. Children's books are larger, four-color and have 32 pages. Cookbooks are wider than they are tall so they will open and lie flat. Travel books are lightweight and easy to carry.

Milt Strong writes and publishes books on square dancing. All his books measure about 4½ x 8 inches. He explains that dancers want a tall, skinny format so they can read the steps and then slip the book into a back pocket.

Your book must look like the rest on its shelf. Do not break out of the mold on your first attempt. If your book is *different*, it will lose credibility. Potential buyers will think you are an amateur and not ready to be a serious author-publisher.

Give your buyer what he or she expects, wants and deserves.

If you want your book to sell like a book, it has to look like a book.

Craft a Short Title

Your title should be easy to remember and easy to say.

The words should relate well to each other. A short title has fewer words a customer can get wrong.

Tom Brokaw's book is titled *The Greatest Generation*, Mitch Albom's book is *Tuesdays with Morrie* and Peter Jennings wrote *The Century*. Keep your title short and snappy.

Books in Print uses a 92-character computer field. Ingram, the big book wholesaler, uses a 30-character field. Try to make your title and subtitle tell most of the story in the first 30 characters.

Books in Print lists all currently available books by title, author and subject but most directories list only by title. If you start your title with the keyword, your book listing will be easier to find. If your book is on how to win high school elections, try to start with the keyword "election." Then your book will be listed alongside other election books.

Your subtitle may be longer and should be more descriptive. Together, the title and subtitle should leave no doubt what the book is about.

Make your title specific, familiar and short.

Your title should be five words or less or people have to use their brains to repeat it.
—Jeff Herman, literary agent.

Beware of Working Titles

Be careful what you make permanent.

Working titles are dangerous. They can become too familiar to us while being misleading or meaningless to potential customers.

Choices: A Teen Woman's Journal for Self-Awareness and Personal Planning was a hot seller but it could not be used in schools unless there was a version for the boys. So the authors, Mindy Bingham, Judy Edmonson and Sandy Stryker, wrote a masculine edition. Working titles ranged from *Choices II*, to *Choices Too*, and even *Son of Choices*. What sounded ridiculous or humorous in the beginning became familiar and sounded fairly good.

Finally, the three authors settled on *Changes,* but found that men did not warm up to the proposed title. After discussions with a number of men, they agreed to change the title to *Challenges: A Teen Man's Journal for Self-Awareness and Personal Planning.* Most men rise to challenges but do not like changes.

http://www.academicinnovations.com

A *working title* is for the manuscript, not necessarily for the book.

Authors, as a rule, are poor judges of titles and often go for the cute or clever rather than the practical.
—**Nat Bodian, author, *How to Choose a Winning Title.***

Hire a Book Cover Designer

Get professional help.

Cover designers work with color and type every day. They know where to place the title and bar code. They not only lay out covers, they work with printers to make sure their design and colors are faithfully reproduced. Designers provide a needed service; they provide more than art.

Robert Howard is the dean of cover artists. In the early 1980s he saw a need and filled it. Now many artists serve the smaller publishers. Robert likes to read much of the text and then try to get the feeling of the book into the cover art.

He says: "The package outside should represent and sell the text inside." rhgd@verinet.com

Do not give too much direction to your graphic artist and stifle the creativity you are paying for. Do not say, "I want yellow with a drawing of . . ." Provide general direction. Provide a model book you like and tell the artist you want your cover to be classy or rustic or one that says mystery. Let the artist give you his or her best interpretation with a *little* of your input.

Spend money on the package.

The most common mistake made by publishers small and large is cutting corners on the cost of covers.
—Robert Erdmann, publishing consultant and past president of the Publishers Marketing Association.

Covers Sell Books

Packaging is everything.

The bookstore browser spends just 8 seconds on the front cover and 15 seconds on the back cover. You must hook them immediately and keep them reading the back cover or they will put the book back on the shelf.

Everyone judges a book by its cover. No one reads the book before they make a buying decision. Consumers do not read it in the store. Sales reps only carry book covers and jackets (books are too heavy) to show bookstore buyers, and wholesalers and distributors say, "Just send us the cover copy." All buying decisions are made on the illustration/design and the sales copy on the outside of the book. Yes, packaging is everything.

Most of Lightbourne's work is done long distance, so when the new client walked in wearing buckskin and natural cotton attire, Gaelyn and Bram Larrick knew that this project would be unique and fun. Matt Richards had written a book on taking raw deerskin and creating beautiful buckskin garments and useful goods, a process that was more of a lifestyle for him.

He had located the cover design company as a result of reading Dan Poynter's *Self-Publishing Manual*, but was still nervous about spending his money on a professionally designed cover.

Matt lived in the wilderness and his way of life didn't require him to earn much money. The cover would cost one-quarter of his entire annual income.

Six months later, he wrote that his book was selling so well in both his niche market and bookstores that his annual income had already increased four to five times over.

http://www.lightbourne.com

Since everyone from the distributor, to wholesalers, to bookstore buyers, to the ultimate customer judges a book by its cover, give them what they need—a compelling cover with art and a sales message that will encourage a buying decision.

Anyone who says 'you can't judge a book by its cover' has never met the category buyer from Barnes & Noble.
— **Terri Lonier, author, *Working Solo*.**

Draft Your Back-Cover Sales Copy First

Do not leave this project to someone else.

To focus on who your customers are and what you plan to share with them, draft your back-cover sales copy before you write the book.

Book cover designers will lay out the package and incorporate the illustration, put it all on disk and send it to the printer; but someone must draft the sales copy. Publishers are notorious for writing weak copy. Do it yourself. Be assertive.

Psychotherapist Pete Buntman wrote a guidebook for parents titled *How to Live With Your Teenager*. The book was selling well but he decided to spruce up the packaging with new cover art and new sales copy on the back. Sales shot up over 50%.
http://www.ADHD.com

Think about your primary audience and list the benefits of your book. Tell the bookstore browser what is inside and how the book will help them. Use the back cover of this book as an outline. Then write your book and deliver on your promises.

Drafting the cover copy will make the book writing easier because you will focus on your readers and have a list of what you plan to tell them.

You can't tell—but you can sell—a book by its cover.
—The Wall Street Journal.

Place Your Photograph Inside

Do not put your photo on the front or back cover.

The covers are prime sales space and there is not much of it. The front cover is your billboard; make it attractive. The back cover is for sales copy; make it convincing. Don't put anything on the covers that will not sell the book.

Unless your face is recognizable because you are a politician, movie star or other high-profile person, leave it off the covers.

Ed Rigsbee is the exception because he worked his photo into the cover message. The jacket of *The Art of Partnering* shows Ed reaching up to hold the wrists of two people shaking hands.

http://speakers.com/rigsbee.html

Your photograph should be in the book. Your readers are investing their time and money in you and many want to know who is talking to them. Put your photo in the front matter on the "About the Author" page. Then write a whole page about yourself.

Forget the ego trips; the covers should be used to sell the book.

Egotism is the anesthetic that dulls the pain of stupidity.
—Frank Leahy, in *Look* magazine, 1955.

Disclaimers

"This book is just one source of information on this subject."

A disclaimer in your book may not completely insulate you from liability, but it might help prove you showed due care in warning the reader of potential dangers.

Some plaintiffs have been successful:

- A publisher was held liable for a defective aviation map that led to a plane crash.
- *Soldier of Fortune* magazine was held liable for publishing an ad for a hit man, which resulted in a murder.

According to Mark Warda (attorney turned publisher) of Sphinx Publishing, these cases involve publishers; he has yet to find a case against authors. Of course, that may be because authors usually are not insured and, therefore, have shallower pockets.

In many cases, both authors and publishers may be protected by the First Amendment guarantees of freedom of expression and freedom of the press.

Some reviewers have noted these disclaimers in their reviews, commenting that the information must be worthless since the author and publisher do not stand behind the advice. We will see who is right years from now when today's books are held to a future standard. Plan ahead; be prepared; include a disclaimer in your front matter.

> *Long-range planning does not deal with future decisions, but with the future of present decisions.*
> **—Peter F. Drucker, Austrian-American management consultant and educator.**

Chapter Seven
Copyright

Copyright is an interesting concept and it isn't very difficult to understand.

Many new authors are preoccupied with two questions:

1. How much of someone else's work may I safely use?
2. How can I protect my work from plagiarists?

Most nonfiction is simply a reformulation of existing ideas and facts derived from research.

> *Plagiarists, at least, have the merit of preservation.*
> **—Benjamin Disraeli (1804–1881), British writer**
> **and prime minister.**

Know How Much You May Borrow

Borrow ideas, *borrow* facts, *but do not* steal *words.*

Copyright covers the author's presentation or *expression*—a sequence or pattern of words. It does not protect *ideas*. If you read and blend the ideas of other authors and put the collective thought into your own words, that is perfectly legal. This is how most nonfiction books are written—from research.

Do not repeat any of the research materials word for word. Some of the material is not yours, so copying could be plagiarism and you would be guilty of copyright infringement. Adapt the ideas from many sources so that your work is not *substantially similar* to any of them.

In *Feist Publications, Inc. v. Rural Telephone Service Company, Inc.*, 111 S.Ct. 1282, 1287–88 (1991), the court held that the name and address listings (facts) taken from a telephone directory were not protected by copyright.

Facts may not be copyrighted either; they are free for anyone to repeat or use in a manuscript.

Copy from one, it's plagiarism; copy from two, it's research.
—Wilson Mizner, screenwriter.

Protect Your Work from Thieves

How can I guard against others stealing my writing?

The moment you create a written Work, it is automatically copyrighted under common law. Once the book is published, you may send two copies to the Copyright Office with the two-page Form TX and $30 to *register* or perfect your copyright.

Some (new) authors copyright their manuscript. Later, when they turn it into a book, they print the original copyright date. This makes the book appear to be old, and that hurts sales.

Most authors wait and send the *finished* book to the Copyright Office for registration.

http://www.loc.gov

A registered copyright only gains the author some extra rights. The difference is between *copyright* and *registered copyright*, not between *not copyrighted* and *copyrighted*. Copyright occurs automatically with creation—when you initially write it.

Publishers rarely steal manuscripts. They are in the publishing business, not the writing business. Manuscripts are cheap and publishers do not even have to pay the authors until months after the books are sold. There is little incentive to rip you off.

> *The instinct of ownership is fundamental in man's nature.*
> **—William James (1842–1910), American philosopher and psychologist.**

Research Your Title

Copyright protects the text, not the title.

One reason book titles may not be copyrighted is that there are too many books and too few words in the language. There are just not enough words to go around.

Research *Books in Print* and *Forthcoming Books in Print* for competing titles. Search an online bookstore database such as the one provided by Amazon.com.

Sometimes two books with the same title are launched in the same year. In 1978, Harper & Row and Knopf both published books titled *Continental Drift*. And in 1984, St. Martins and Knopf both published books titled *Pearl*.

Make sure your title does not even *sound* like the title of an existing book. Your promotional efforts may result in sales of the other book.

Do not waste your efforts competing for attention for a book with a same title. You want to spend your time selling your book, not competing with another book.

You may protect your title by trademarking it but that is expensive and rarely done.

One particular problem we have at the Baltimore Public Library is with similar titles. Almost every season there are two or three popular titles that are similar to one another. This leads to scrambled title requests. We have to be aware of these titles and their differences so we can interpret these requests and direct inquirers to the right title.
—Nora Wallenson, librarian.

Chapter Eight
Finding an Agent
Finding a Publisher

Once your manuscript is complete, it is time to decide how it should be published. You may approach a large, general (New York) publisher; a mid-size niche publisher; an agent; a vanity press (not a good choice); or publish yourself.

Everyone's situation is different. The solution for one person is not the best solution for all. Consider your five T's: Time, Temperament, Talent, Training and Territory.

If you are looking for an agent or a publisher, research and get to know what kinds of books they have represented or published in the past.

To speed the process, make more money and keep control of their work, some authors do not spend time on proposals. They self-publish in hardcover and then send the book to agents and publishers offering the softcover, mass-market paperback, foreign language, electronic and audio rights.

The best and most businesslike way to write for money—and consistent publication—is to find out what editors want and try·to produce it.
—Kay Haugaard, author, *No Place*.

Find an Agent or Publisher Before You Write

Prepare a book proposal.

Savvy authors sell their idea for a book before they write it. They draft a proposal and send it to agents and publishers. When you think about it, that is a much more efficient way to conduct a writing business. Why spend months or years writing on spec?

Historically, the advance was paid to support the author while the book was being written. The author would propose a book to the publisher and the publisher would give the author an advance against anticipated future royalties.

Even self-publishers should draft proposals to assess the size of the market, uncover the competition and plan the direction for the book.

Use the proposal to sell both you and the idea—and make your proposal irresistible.

Professionals sell, then write, while amateurs write, then try to sell.

—Gordon Burgett, author, *Sell & Resell Your Magazine Articles*.

Go Directly to the Publisher

Prepare a query letter.

If you write directly to the editor or publisher, you may be able to eliminate the proposal step and maybe the agent. About 20% of the manuscripts purchased by larger publishers come from authors, not agents.

"Query" comes from "inquiry" and asks if the editor or publisher might be interested in seeing the proposal or manuscript.

Your query letter should cover four areas: the subject matter/idea, why you should write it, what else is in print about it and how your book differs. Tell them who you are and why people care (or will care) about the subject matter.

Lisa Roberts finished her manuscript. She planned to self-publish, so she joined a publishing listserv to learn more about book production and promotion. Her questions referred to her title: *How to Raise a Family and a Career Under One Roof: A Parent's Guide to Home Business*.

Dennis Damp at Bookhaven Press expressed an interest, so she replied with a query letter, describing her project from concept to competition, her target market and expected media interest in the subject matter. That was all he needed. He wanted to see the manuscript; a proposal would not be necessary.

The book received a lot of media attention and is going into a second printing.

http://www.en-parent.com

The query must be well written and sell your idea. The recipient will be evaluating your writing style as well as the project. It should be a couple of pages with attachments. Enclose an annotated table of contents, a one-page synopsis, and a reference sheet listing where you are obtaining your information (books, articles, case studies, interviews, etc.). Think of a query as a mini proposal.

> *Your manuscript must do battle with a pile of others sitting on the editor's desk.*
> **—Betsy Mitchell, editor-in-chief of Warner Books'**
> **science fiction/fantasy line, Aspect.**

Understand Agents

Approach the gatekeepers.

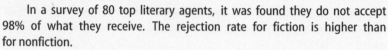

Many larger publishers prefer to have manuscripts filtered through agents.

Agents provide three services for their 15%: (1) they find a publisher by matching your manuscript to the publisher; (2) they negotiate the contract; and (3) they may help develop the manuscript. Most agents today will require you to draft a book proposal for submission to the publishers. Proposal writing is usually a lengthy and time-consuming process.

In a survey of 80 top literary agents, it was found they do not accept 98% of what they receive. The rejection rate for fiction is higher than for nonfiction.

The big publishers continue to consolidate. There are only about 20 large- and medium-sized trade publishers that will give an advance large enough to make a 15% commission meaningful. Divisions within the same house will not bid against each other. It is getting tougher to be an agent; they are prisoners of the system.

Literary agents are 85% hope and 15% commission.

I am absolutely convinced that every author of large and varied output ought to put the whole of his affairs into the hands of a good agent, and that every such author who fails to do so loses money by his omission.
—Arnold Bennett (1867–1931), English novelist and playwright.

Find the *Right* Agent

Most agents specialize.

Some literary agents have a passion and a track record for certain kinds of books: cooking, travel, children's, business, parenting and so on. To find the right agent for your manuscript, simply match it to the agent. See the various agent directories and ask around. Locate and call authors of works similar to yours. Ask who their agent is.

Agent Patti Breitman (John Gray, *Men are From Mars,* and Richard Carlson, *Don't Sweat the Small Stuff*) is a confirmed and renowned vegetarian. When she was new to the business, she attended many vegetarian conferences and let people know she was looking for manuscripts. After she sold a few, the word spread in vegetarian circles.

Now Patti represents the founder of People for the Ethical Treatment of Animals, Ingrid Newkirk (*You Can Save the Animals*); the founder of Physicians' Committee for Responsible Medicine, Neal Barnard, MD (*Foods That Fight Pain* and *Food for Life*); the fourth-generation cattle rancher turned vegetarian who got Oprah sued, Howard Lyman (*Mad Cowboy*); and several others.

Today, Patti receives several queries and proposals for vegetarian books. Because she is not taking on many new clients, Patti must sometimes decline the chance to work with even the best vegetarian authors. But she will suggest other agents and encourage the writers to persevere, because she shares their passion.

At writers' conferences, try this nonthreatening way of approaching agents: Do not ask an agent to read your manuscript. Instead, put them in a more objective position by saying, "You are an agent and know most of the other agents. I realize agents have a track record in certain types of work. Which agents would you recommend for this manuscript?" You will be astonished at the positive reaction you get.

It's harder for a new writer to get an agent than a publisher.
—Roger Straus, president, Farrar, Straus & Giroux.

Expect Rejection

Great writers have their work returned too.

Remember, Moses climbed the mountain, lifted up the two tablets of stone and received the Ten Commandments. Then he returned to the people.

You have heard all that before, but do you know the rest of the story? A couple of days later, Moses climbed back up that mountain. The thunder roared, the lightning flashed, the clouds parted, the skies opened wide and the face of the Lord appeared. A voice said: "Moses, why are you back here so soon?"

Moses replied: "I did what you said. I carried the tablets down to the people. They are sending the tablets back with this note:

> Thank you for your submission, which we regret
> has been found unsuited to our current needs."

Stephen King had three novels rejected before Doubleday bought *Carrie*. Sam Sinclair Baker had 17 publishers reject his *Scarsdale Diet*. Richard Bach's agent said, "Look, no one cares about a talking seagull right now." Never be discouraged. Even the best writers are sometimes rejected.

Be persistent. Editors change; tastes change; editorial markets change. Too many beginning writers give up too easily.
—John Jakes, North and South.

Be Persistent

Explain it again, Sam.

Agents specialize, publishers specialize, and industry people have different (narrow) interests.

In late 1989, Jeff Davidson sent a proposal to Rick Horgan at Warner Books for a book titled *A Layman's Guide for Saving the Planet*. This was a book that would walk readers through their homes, room by room, and show them how to be environmentally responsible.

Horgan sent back a rejection letter, saying that he thought the proposal had merit, but that the editors at Warner felt that no one in America realistically would change their "cozy, comfortable lifestyles."

Four months later, Earthworks Group published *50 Simple Things You Can Do to Save the Earth* and it became a 3.5 million-copy worldwide best seller endorsed at the highest levels of business and government, including the White House. Several other environmental books quickly followed, with many of them doing very well.

http://www.BreathingSpace.com

You know more about your subject than just about anyone else because you have done the research. You may be assuming that everyone is as familiar with the subject as you are.

Just because editors have *life-and-death power* does not mean they are always right. Some people just do not get it.

Ask yourself, "Are they rejecting the manuscript or the idea?" Perhaps you have not made the project sound exciting or promising.

A professional writer is an amateur who didn't quit.
—Richard Bach, *A Gift of Wings,* **1974.**

Find the *Right* Publisher

Do your homework.

The secret to finding a publisher is simple, yet very few writers do it: *match your manuscript to the publisher.*

Major publishers specialize in one or two niche markets. They know their subjects, want to know about all the books in their subject area, and do not have to send your manuscript out to a reader for evaluation. They also know how to reach the potential buyer and can jump-start your sales by plugging your book into their existing distribution system to specialty shops, associations and events.

We all have heard of the author who was turned down by 34 publishers before being "discovered." He or she was turned down for sending off an unsolicited manuscript.

Some larger publishers get 3,000 to 4,000 manuscripts every week. They have someone who opens the packages and inserts the contents into the return envelope. These authors are being *rejected* without being *read*.

To find these specialized publishers, visit a couple of larger bookstores. Check the shelf where your book will be and look for books as close to yours as possible. Match potential buyers: Would the potential buyer of books on this shelf be interested in your book?

Then go to your public library and consult *Books in Print*, a multivolumed reference that lists all the books currently available for sale. Look up the publishers' telephone numbers and addresses in the last volume.

When you call a medium-sized, specialized publisher, you will often get through to the top person. They know what you are talking about and they are usually very interested. They will be able to tell you instantly whether the proposed book will fit into their line.

To contact the right person at a larger publishing company (generally, if you have heard of it, it is "larger"), you will have to get by the "Call Prevention Department"; you will need a name to get past the switchboard. Check the acknowledgments in similar books; authors often reference their editor. Then look them up in *Literary Market Place* at the library.

Call the editor (or the publisher in a smaller house), reference the similar title they published, and ask if they would like to see your manuscript. Then you will have someone to send your work to. Do not take "no" for an answer. If you are turned down, ask for a referral. These editors know the editors at other houses who specialize in their field. Then call the second editor, using the first as a reference.

Authors do detailed research on the subject matter but seldom do any on which publishing house is appropriate for their work.
—**Walter W. Powell, editor, author,** *Getting Into Print.*

Don't Sign the First Contract

The big print giveth and the small print taketh away.

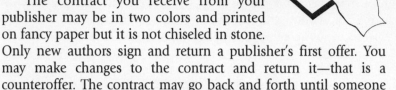

The contract you receive from your publisher may be in two colors and printed on fancy paper but it is not chiseled in stone. Only new authors sign and return a publisher's first offer. You may make changes to the contract and return it—that is a counteroffer. The contract may go back and forth until someone accepts it.

I took a distressing telephone call from an author who had just received a contract from a large New York publisher. There were a total of 21 items in the contract she didn't like or didn't understand. After discussing some of them, I suggested she call her editor. Better communication was certainly required here.

She called back two days later, both astonished and delighted. When she asked about the first paragraph in question, the editor said, "That's okay; you can have it." She got what she wanted on the next paragraph in question too. On one other paragraph that concerned her, the editor said something like "Well, that sounds like *this* but in the book trade it really means *that*, so it isn't a big issue."

The result: she got 19 out of the 21 things she asked for. So contract discussions do not mean pulling the wool over the eyes of your publisher. This was a win-win negotiation.

http://www.ParaPublishing.com

Take the contract to a *book* attorney (not just any attorney, not a contract attorney and not a media attorney). When it comes to literary properties and money, you need professional help. And make a counteroffer.

Remember, all of this is negotiable. The contract looks like it is set in stone when you review it, but anything can be scratched out or inked in. If you want more books, a better discount or more help with marketing, negotiate for it. You may not get it, but you never know if you don't ask.
—**Joe "Mr. Fire" Vitale, author,** *Cyber Writing.*

Never Pay a Publisher

If it sounds too good to be true, check the real cost.

Vanity or subsidy presses almost always accept a manuscript for publication and usually do so with a glowing review letter. They don't make any promises regarding sales, and usually the book sells fewer than 100 copies. The vanity publisher doesn't have to sell any books because the author has already paid for the work.

Vanity publishers produce around 6,000 titles each year. Under a typical arrangement, the author pays much more than the printing bill, receives 40% of the retail price of the books sold and 80% of the subsidiary rights, if sold. Many vanity publishers will charge you $10,000 to $30,000 to publish your book, depending upon its number of pages and binding. It is hard to understand why an author would pay $20,000 when he or she can pay a printer a quarter of the price.

Soma Vira, PhD, paid $44,000 to have three of her books produced by a well-known subsidy publisher. She received 250 books but could not verify how many were printed and suspects they made very few for stock. The books were not properly edited, typeset, proofed or manufactured. Distributors, bookstores and reviewers refused to consider books from this and other vanity presses. Her books cost her $176 each and she had to start over.
http://www.SpaceLinkBooks.com

The review copies sent to columnists by a subsidy publisher usually go straight into the circular file. Reviewers are wary of vanity presses because they know that little attention was paid to the editing of the book. Further, they realize there will be little promotional effort and that the book will not be available to readers in the stores. Therefore, the name of the vanity publisher on the spine of the book is a *kiss of death*.

Pay to have your book *printed*. Do not pay to have it *published*.

Legitimate publishers don't have to look for business.
—Linda Hasselstrom, author, *The Book Book: A Publishing Handbook for Beginners and Others*.

Consider Publishing Yourself

If you self-publish, you will make more money, get to press sooner and keep control of your work.

My first real book was *The Parachute Manual: A Technical Treatise on Aerodynamic Decelerators*. It was 8½ x 11 with 2,000 illustrations and 590 pages. It did not take long to find that publishers were not interested in a large technical niche book. I also found out that if I had sold out, the low royalty rate would not repay me for the eight years of work in writing it.

Worse, no publisher would know where to sell such a manual. This was not a bookstore-type book. It had to be sold to parachute manufacturers, parachute lofts and skydiving instructors. I knew how to find them. By self-publishing, I made more money.

My second book was titled *Hang Gliding: The Basic Handbook of Skysurfing*. I saw the movement coming, loved to fly, and wrote the first book on the subject. From idea to a printed book took just 4½ months. Since it takes most large publishers 18 months to turn a manuscript into a book and get it to the stores, I had the only book on the subject for almost two years. By the time a competing title was published, I had sold over 30,000 copies and owned the territory. By self-publishing, I got to press sooner.

A few books later, I teamed up with Frisbee® expert Mark Danna to write *The Frisbee Player's Handbook*. The gimmick was to make the book circular. I had them punched out 8.7" in diameter with a short 5.5" spine. Then we packaged the book in a custom-imprinted 119 gm. Frisbee disk. The unique book was reviewed everywhere. No publisher would have produced a book like this. By self-publishing, I kept control of my work.

http://www.ParaPublishing.com

Only two people make money on a book: the printer and the investor.

Chapter Nine
Book Promotion

Around 100,000 titles are published each year in the U.S. That amounts to nearly 300 per day. Over 1.3 million books are in print or currently available. To display them all, a bookstore would need five miles of shelf space. Most stores stock 40,000 to 80,000 titles.

It does not matter whether you sell out to a large publisher or self-publish—the author must do the promotion. Everyone in the book industry has a role: authors write, publishers publish, printers print, authors promote and bookstores sell. Authors promote? They must, because no one else does.

The contract you receive from your publisher guarantees you a percentage of the price of every book sold. No one guarantees the number of books that will end up in the hands of buyers.

Do not be lulled into a false sense of security by thinking your publisher will promote your book. Your publisher will get your book into bookstores but you must get the buyers into the stores. Your book will be on the shelf for just four months. If it does not sell well, it will be pulled off and replaced with another front list recent book.

Just as a parent's responsibilities do not end with giving birth, an author's do not end with publication. The child must be raised and the book must be promoted. Fortunately, your book is not a 20-year commitment and you do not have to send it to college.

> *My experience has been that the big New York publishers do next to nothing to promote their books. I asked an editor at Berkeley what they did to market their 200 books a month and she said 'Nothing.' Then she added, 'Well, we list them in our catalog.'*
> **—Joe "Mr. Fire" Vitale, author.**

Don't Host Autograph Parties

When my parents taught me not to write in books, they did not know they were raising an author who would autograph them.

An autograph party says, "Come and appreciate me (and buy a book)"; a seminar says, "Come on down and I will give you something free (information) that will improve your life." Always think of the *benefit* to the potential customer. How can you lure them out of the house and down to the store?

Patricia Bragg (Health-Science Publishing) publishes health and fitness books. To promote her mini seminar at a local bookshop in Santa Barbara, she posted handbills in all the local health food stores. Then she did a postcard mailing to her customer list within a 50-mile (driving) radius. The store was packed and she was on for over four hours—until closing time. The store sold out on many of her titles and gave out rain checks.
http://www.bragg.com

Autographings are not a party in your honor—you and your book are not even known yet. Your appearance is a promotional opportunity requiring hard work.

Book signings are a form of product promotion not available to producers of other goods or services. Bookstores, both chain and independent, stage events to attract potential customers into their stores. Authors are the draw.

These mini seminars may lead to longer ones for other groups at other locations—for money.

Never do an autographing; *always offer a* mini seminar. *Attract buyers to your autograph parties.*
—Terri Lonier, author, *Working Solo*.

Hit the Airwaves

Exploit the inexpensive way to sell books.

According to Bradley Communications, more than 10,200 guests appear on some 4,250 local news, interview and talk shows across the U.S each day. And about 95% of the guests do not have recognizable names.

Radio and television talk shows need interesting guests to attract listeners and viewers. Most people think that authors are experts and celebrities, so most of the guests booked on these shows are authors. Your book is actually your entrée to the airwaves.

A mention or an interview on any show can sell books, but the very best is Oprah Winfrey's show. Many authors have seen their books climb to the best-seller lists due to an appearance there.

Advertising products on the air is expensive, and since people are skeptical of advertising, they tend to tune it out. Interviews, however, are *editorial* matter. People listen to editorial matter. Interviews are more effective than advertising and they are free.

The six most important words in book promotion are: 'Nice to see you again, Oprah.'

Consider a Publicist

Hire a gunslinger.

Many publishers suggest that authors hire a book publicist at their own expense. Way back in 1988, *The Wall Street Journal* ran an article titled "Authors Invest in Their Own Publicists to Ensure Books Are Not Overlooked." The article began with "Bestselling books are made, not born."

Fred Klein, former executive editor and vice-president of Bantam books, says: "Large houses may have only four or five publicists in their department. They usually come in at entry level and are overworked and underpaid to cover an average of 12 authors published each month. Realistically, only a couple out of the total get much attention."

Most independent book publicists charge $2,000 to $5,000 a month, and it usually takes six months or more just to lay the groundwork for an effective publicity campaign.

Publicists should get involved early. If the book is languishing in the bookstores, it is too late.

> *Hiring a publicist isn't a vanity; it's a realistic commercial decision.*
> **—Paul Cowan, author, *Mixed Blessings*.**

Give Books Away

Plant a book and grow much fruit.

Give free copies of your book to anyone who influences people such as book reviewers and opinion molders.

Harvey Mackay sent free copies of his new book, *Pushing the Envelope, All the Way to the Top*, to each of the 3,800 members of the National Speakers Association. These opinion molders address and influence millions of people annually.

http://www.mackay.com

Review copies are the least expensive and most effective way to promote books. A book costs $1 or $2 to print, around $1 to ship and maybe 30 cents for the shipping bag. Space advertising in a magazine may cost $1,500 or more. That ad would have to bring in a lot of orders to pay off—experience says it won't.

It costs far less to send books to reviewers and other opinion molders than to buy advertising space. When in doubt, ship it out.

A book reviewer is usually a barker before the door of a publisher's circus.
—Austin O'Malley.

Be Grateful for a Bad Review

A bad review is better than no review.

Any review is a good review because it results in *ink*. This exposure will bring in orders. As John Kremer says: "No one remembers the negativity of the review but they do remember the title of the book."

Author Andrew Greeley comments, "Many book reviewers are mean spirited. Even if a reviewer likes a book, he or she must find fault and write snide and/or patronizing little asides about the author's character or motives that demonstrate the reviewer's intellectual and moral superiority."

While some readers may be discouraged by a bad review from buying your book, other people will see through the review and buy the book because the subject interests them.

Few new products get the free publicity showered on books. Authors, publishers and booksellers owe a debt of thanks to reviewers. Hope for good ink and be grateful for bad ink. Ink is ink.

Just write the best book you are capable of writing; then, take solace in the fact that most people do not buy books on the basis of any review they actually read.
—Steve Wasserman, book editor, *The Los Angeles Times*.

Ask for Testimonials

Put words in their mouths.

Testimonials, forewords, endorsements and quotations or "blurbs" sell books because word-of-mouth is one of the most powerful forces in marketing. Anything *you* say about your book is self-serving, but words from *another* person are not. In fact, when readers see the quotation marks, it shifts their attitude and they become more receptive.

Harvey Mackay placed 44 testimonials in *Swim With the Sharks*; he had endorsements from everyone from Billy Graham to Robert Redford. Did these luminaries buy a book and write unsolicited testimonials? Of course not. Mackay asked for the words of praise.
http://www.mackay.com

Your mission is to get the highest placed, most influential opinion molders talking about your book. You have more control than you think over whom you quote, what they say and how you use their words. Testimonials are not difficult to get.

To help your endorser come up with a pertinent, targeted testimonial, send the manuscript with a letter, saying: "I know you are very busy. I was thinking of something like this . . ." Then draft a suggested blurb for them.

Most testimonials are superficial, teach the reader nothing and lack credibility.
—Ron Richards, President, Venture Network.

Appendix

Your Action Plan

Here is your book road map. Photocopy this page and post it above your desk. Check off each stage as you complete it.

☐ Research your subject/idea, competition and title.

☐ Draft your covers (and select a working title).

☐ Set up your binder with dividers and pages, and slip the proposed covers into the outside pockets.

☐ Get a *model* book.

☐ Research your topic. Gather information.

☐ First draft. Get what you have onto the hard disk and into the binder.

☐ Second draft. Content edit. Research and fill in the blanks.

☐ Third draft. Peer review. Send out the chapters for feedback.

☐ Fourth draft. Copy edit. Clean up the punctuation, grammar and style. Fact checking.

☐ Publishing choice: Approach a publisher or self-publish.

    ☐ Typesetting

    ☐ Proofreading

    ☐ Printing

☐ Promotion: Review copies, news releases, autograph parties and radio/TV interviews.

Writing Resources

Books

Writing Nonfiction: Turning Thoughts into Books by Dan Poynter. $14.95. Para Publishing. Tel: 800-PARAPUB; info@ParaPublishing.com

Is There a Book Inside You? Writing Alone or With a Collaborator by Dan Poynter and Mindy Bingham. $14.95. Para Publishing. Tel: 800-PARAPUB; info@ParaPublishing.com

Writing Your Book: A Quick & Easy Recipe for Writing Your Nonfiction Book by Dan Poynter. A 75-minute videotape. $29.95. Tel: 800-PARAPUB; info@ParaPublishing.com

The Self-Publishing Manual: How to Write, Print and Sell Your Own Book by Dan Poynter. The complete manual on book production, marketing and distribution. 464 pages. $19.95. Tel: 800-PARAPUB; info@ParaPublishing.com

Getting Your Book Published: Inside Secrets of a Successful Author by Robert W. Bly. 210 pages. $14.95. Roblin Press. 800-874-9083.

How to Get Happily Published by Judith Appelbaum. 317 pages. $13.95. HarperPerennial.

The Silver Pen: Starting a Profitable Writing Business From a Lifetime of Experience by Alan Canton. 376 pages. $22.95. Adams-Blake Publishing. 916-962-9296. abpub@ns.net

You Can Become a Columnist by Charlotte Digregorio. 332 pages. $13.95. Tel: 503-228-6649.

Contests

For more than 400 contests, see the list in *Literary Market Place* available at the reference desk of your public library. Also see *The Complete Guide to Literary Contests* at http://www.prometheusbooks.com

Information

For a free Book Writing Information Kit, contact Para Publishing, PO Box 8206, Santa Barbara, CA 93118-8206. Tel: 800-PARAPUB; info@ParaPublishing.com

Free documents available from the Para Publishing web site: http://ParaPublishing.com

112: *Poynter's Secret List of Book Promotion Contacts.* Names and numbers for ABI, LC, CIP, ISBN and more; list of pre-publication reviewers; list of directories you should be listed in and over 50 places to send your book for review. 8 pages.

114: *Inside Book Writing.* An instant report of little-known and rarely understood secrets every author should know. 7 pages.

115: *Inside Book Publishing.* An instant report of little-known and rarely understood secrets every publisher should know. 8 pages.

116: *Book Cover Layout.* Paint-by-the-numbers instructions on how to lay out your covers. The wrapper sells the book; your covers must follow this outline to be successful. 2 pages.

135: *Speaking on Book Writing.* Dan Poynter is available to speak to your writers' conference. Descriptive brochure with rates. 5 pages.

137: *Consulting with Dan Poynter.* You may speak with Dan Poynter one on one over the telephone or in person at your office or his. Descriptive brochure with rates. 2 pages.

140: *Resources on Writing and Publishing Specific Types of Books.* An instant report listing books, magazines, newsletters, pamphlets and associations dealing with specific areas of book writing and publishing. For example, there are three books on how to write, produce and market cookbooks, four on travel, eight on life stories, etc. 8 pages.

142: *Mailing Lists for Promoting Books.* A brochure describing more than 100 lists of reviewers who want to write about your books. 2 pages.

155: *Books That Were Originally Self-Published.* Many bestsellers were published by their authors. A list. 1 page.

156: *Book Titles That Were Changed.* Many bestsellers began with other titles. A list. 1 page.

250: A list of suppliers of services to the publishing industry with addresses and numbers. 4 pages.

167: Publishing workshops in Santa Barbara. A two-day marketing/promoting/distributing seminar at Dan Poynter's home/office. Description, rates and an application. 2 pages.

Web Sites of Interest to Writers

A Cappela Publishing
Lectures, Writing Seminars, Books & Tapes
http://www.acappela.com

Allworth Press
Books for the Creative Professional
http://www.allworth.com

Amazon.com
An online bookstore. Good database for researching titles.
http://www.Amazon.com

Barnes & Noble
http://www.barnesandnoble.com

Big Yellow Pages
http://www.bigyellow.com

Borders
http://www.borders.com

Bookwire (links to many author web sites)
http://www.bookwire.com

Book Zone
http://www.bookzone.com

Children's Writing Resource Center
http://www.write4kids.com/index.html

Cyberwall Writer's Resources
http://www.nb.net/~downs/downswr.htm

Dictionary Links
http://www.yahoo.com/reference/dictionaries/

Elements of Style by William Strunk Jr.
http://www.columbia.edu/acis/bartleby/strunk

Fatbrain Ematter
http://www.fatbrain.com/ematter

1stBooks.com. Electronic books.
http://www.1stBooks.com

iTools! Research site.
http://www.itools.com

Inkspot Writer's Forum
http://www.inkspot.com

International Women's Writing Guild
http://www.iwwg.com

Internet Public Library
http://www.ipl.org

Media Research Center
http://www.mediaresearch.org

My Virtual Reference Desk
http://www.refdesk.com/facts.html

The New York Times
http://www.nytimes.com/books

Para Publishing
http://www.ParaPublishing.com

Reed Reference Publishing. *Marquis Who's Who, Books Out of Print,* etc.
http://www.reedref.com

Small Publishers, Artists and Writers Network (SPAWN)
http://www.spawn.org

Title Net. Search title information.
http://www.titlenet.com

Virginia Tech Online Writing Lab.
http://www.athena.english.vt.edu

Writers Edge. Industry news and resources.
http://www.nashville,net/~edge

Writers Guild of America
http://www.wga.org/

Writers Net. List of agents.
http://www.writers.net

Writer's Resources
http://www.interlog.com/books.html

Xlibris. Print-On-Demand Books
http://xlibris.com

Writers' Conferences

Maui Writers Conference (Labor Day weekend), PO Box 1118, Kihei, HI 96753. Tel: 808-879-0061. Writers@maui.net; http://www.mauiwriters.com

Santa Barbara Writers Conference (third week in June), Mary and Barnaby Conrad, PO Box 304, Carpinteria, CA 93014. Tel: 805-684-2250.

See *Writers Conferences: An Annual Guide to Literary Conferences.* Writer's Digest Books, 1507 Dana Avenue, Cincinnati, OH 45207.
Tel: 513-531-2222; writersdigest@fwpubs.com

The Guide to Writers Conferences:
http://www.shawguides.com/writing

Index

Advances   116
Agents, finding   115, 116, 118, 119
Albom, Mitch   104
Allen, Fred   53
Allen, Markus   71
Anderson, Karen   79
Anecdotes   39
Anthologies, writing   82
Auden, W.H.   81
Audio   89
Authority   57
Autograph parties   128

Bach, Richard   77, 120, 121
Baker, Sam Sinclair   120
Baldwin, James   143
Barnard, Fred R.   41
Barrie, James Sir   24
Bayle, Pierre   73
Bennett, Arnold   118
Bennett, Hal Zina   70
Best writing   20
Bible   82
Binder   101
Bingham, Mindy   66, 105
Blanchard, Ken   32
Bly, Bob   74
Bodian, Nat   13, 105
Bohr, Niels   32
Booher, Dianna   20, 42
Book doctor   36
Book length   23
Bragg, Patricia   53, 128
Breitman, Patti   119
Brenner Info. Group   12, 35, 102
Brokaw, Tom   104
Brown, Andrea   78
Brown, Rita Mae   47
Bullen, Martha M.   61
Bulwer-Lytton, E.G.   22

Buntman, Pete   108
Burgett, Gordon   24, 81, 85
Burrus, Dan   88
Butts, Rick   55

Canton, Alan   22
Capote, Truman   16
Carlyle, Thomas   93
Chapman, Bruce   45
Chapman, John Jay   83
Charles, Leslie   100
Chicken Soup   46, 79
Children, writing for   78
Chiropractor   86
Choate, Rufus   58
Choices   105
Christie, Agatha   30, 101
Clark, Dan   46
Clay, Patricia   74
Cohn, Leigh   23
Collaboration   30
Colquitt, Harriet Ross   80
Colton, Charles Caleb   15, 68
Column writing   83, 84
Compelling writing   22
Competition   67
Computer   43
Conferences, writers'   100
Contracts, book   124
Cookbooks, writing   80
Copy editor   35
Copyright   63, 112, 113
Cormier, Robert   26
Cossman, Joe   67
Côté, Dick   36
Covers   106, 107, 108
Cowan, Paul   130
Credibility   55
Crisp, Quentin   51
Crosby, Bing   49

Davidson, Jeffrey P.   87, 121
Deadlines   47
Dictation software   44
Disclaimer   110
Disraeli, Benjamin   111
Downs, Robert B.   60
Dragon Software   44
Drucker, Peter F.   110

Edmonson, Judy   105
Edwards, Paul & Sarah   14
Electronic rights   92
Elovson, Allana   78
Email   31
Embree, Mary   95
Emmett, Rita   18
Erdmann, Robert   106
Evans, Nancy   88
Experience   74, 98

Fact checking   34
Fame   52
Family, writing about   77
Fans   53
Feedback   49
Finishing   48
First draft   26
Foreign rights   90
Fortune   59
Fourth draft   35
France, Anatole   54
Franklin, Benjamin   38, 42
Freeman, Rich & Sue   75
Freud, Sigmund   79
Freund, James   14
Frost, Robert   75
Frye, Northrop   66

Galbraith, John Kenneth   28
Gandhi, Mahatma   13
Gardner, Bud   34
Gates, Bill   63
Genesis   91

Ghostwriters   25
Glass, Andrea   29
Glenn, Peggy & Gary   56
Grafton, Sue   11, 13
Greeley, Andrew   132
Gross, Scott   97

Haertig, Evelyn   58
Halberstam, David   10
Hall, Lindsey   23
Halpern, Frances   47, 83, 84
Harper, Tro   45
Harvey, Christine   90
Hasselstrom, Linda   125
Haugaard, Kay   115
Hazards   56
Help   24, 32
Herman, Jeff   104
Hobby, writing about   76
Horn, Sam   19
Horowitz, Shel   48
Hours, selling   64
Howard, Robert   106
Humor   40
Hunter, Cynthia   52

Iacocca, Lee   25, 51
IBM   44
Illustrations   41
Inspiration   61
Interruptions   11

Jacobs, Joel   31
Jakes, John   120
James, William   113
Jesus   39
Johnson, Bob   53
Johnson, Doug   62
Johnson, Samuel   96
Journey, the writing   95
Jowett, Benjamin   63

Kamoroff, Bernard   49

Kearns, Gail   12, 28
King Jr., Martin Luther   13
King, Stephen   120
Kirsch, Jonathan   92
Kissinger, Henry   56
Klein, Fred   130
Kluger, Richard   52
Knievel, Evel   55
Knowledge   62
Krantz, Judith   11

Lamott, Anne   27
Larrick, Gaelyn & Bram   107
Larsen, Michael   61
Leahy, Frank   109
Legacy, your   58
Leonard, Elmore   29
Leonardo da Vinci   93
Lernout and Hauspie   44
Lightbourne Images   107
Locating readers   72
Lonier, Terri   107, 128

Machlin, Milt   40
Mackay, Harvey   51, 131, 133
Maeno, Itoko   37
Maloney, Roy   41
Manchester, William   95
Marquis, Don   84
Martin, Paul Raymond   17, 100
Maurer, Mary   85
Mayhar, Ardath   99
McGinley, Phyllis   76
Meir, Golda   64
Miller, Cynthia   33
Miller, Henry   69
Millman, Dan   17
Mission, your   60
Mitchell, Betsy   117
Mizner, Wilson   112
Model book   102
Money   59

Montaigne, Michel de   82
Moses   120
Mother Nature   37

Naisbitt, John   65
Nathan, Jan   99
Newman, Dan   44
Newton, Ray   16
Nimble, being   73
Nixon, Richard M.   25
Nom de plume   54
Nonfiction v. fiction   70
Nulty, Peter   43

O'Malley, Austin   131
One field, staying in   86
Orwell, George   67

Page eighteen   10
Page turner   10
Paine, Penny   96
Pascal, Blaise   29
Pen names   54
Pfeifer, Diane   73
Photo of author   109
Pinskey, Raleigh   89
Plaut, Tom   39
Powell, Lawrence Clark   11
Powell, Walter W.   123
Poynter, Jim   54
Practice   45, 46
Precise, being   16
Pro CD   77
Procrastination   18
Products   64
Promotion, book   127
Proofreader   37
Proposal, book   116
Pseudonyms   54
Publicist, book   130
Publisher, finding   115, 116, 117,
                               122
Pulitzer, Joseph   39

Puzo, Mario 33

Query 117
Quotations 38

Radio & TV 129
Rae, Donna 60
Raphael, Maryanne 12, 30
Real estate 65
Recycling work 88
Rejection 120
Research 93, 94, 96, 97, 99, 114
Reviews, book 132
Rewriting 28
Richards, Matt 107
Richards, Ron 133
Rigsbee, Ed 109
Roberts, Lisa 117
Rooney, Andy 80
Roth, Philip 37

Salk, Jonas 21
Sanders, Darcie 61
Scuba 72
Sculley, John 51
Second draft 27
Secret, keeping manuscript 33
Sedge, Michael 31
Self-publishing 126
Selling 17
Sheehan, Bill 37
Sinclair, Judit 89
Smith, Sidney J. 94
Spock, Benjamin 62
Stapleton, Cy 97
Stedman, Karen 34
Stephens, Harold 40
Straus, Roger 119
Strong, Milt 103
Stryker, Sandy 105
Sugarman, Joe 43, 45
Synagogue, burning of 22

Targ, William 35
Testimonials 133
Third draft 32
Tight writing 29
Time to write 12, 13, 15, 42
Titles 104, 105, 114
Tracy, Brian 64
Trade magazines 85
Travel writing 81

Untermeyer, Louis 59

Value of information 65
Vanity publishers 125
ViaVoice 44
Vira, Soma 125
Vitale, Joe 55, 57, 58, 62, 124, 127
Vlasak, Weldon 26

Wall Street Journal, The 108
Wallenson, Nora 114
Walters, Dottie 82
Warda, Mark 110
Wasserman, Steve 132
Web, World Wide 97
Werner, Doug 76
Whitman, Walt 72
Wilde, Oscar 70
Williams, Randall 50
Williamson, Bonnie 38
Winfrey, Oprah 129
Wolk, Gloria 57
Women, writing for 79
Writer's block 14
Writer's Digest 13

Zinsser, William K. 40
Zobel, Louise Purwin 94

"The world is before you, and you need not take it or leave it as it was when you came in."
—James Baldwin (1924–1987), novelist and essayist.

◥⧫◣◥⧫◣ *Quick Order Form*

🖨 **Fax orders:** (805) 968-1379. Send this form.

☎ **Telephone orders:** Call 1(800) PARAPUB toll free, (727-2782). Have your credit card ready.

💻 **email orders**: orders@ParaPublishing.com.

🖥 **Postal orders:** Para Publishing, Dan Poynter, PO Box 8206-146, Santa Barbara, CA 93118-8206, USA. Telephone: (805) 968-7277

Please send the following Books, Disks or Reports. I understand that I may return any of them for a full refund—for any reason, no questions asked.

_____

_____

_____

Please send more FREE information on:

☐ Other books, ☐ Speaking/Seminars, ☐ Mailing lists, ☐ Consulting

Name: _____

Address: _____

City: _____ State: _____ Zip: _____ – _____

Telephone: _____

email address: _____

Sales tax: Please add 7.75% for products shipped to California addresses.

Shipping by air:
US: $4 for the first book or disk and $2.00 for each additional product.
International: $9 for 1st book or disk: $5 for each additional product (estimate).

Payment: ☐ Cheque ☐ Credit card:
☐ Visa ☐ MasterCard ☐ Optima ☐ AMEX ☐ Discover

Card number: _____

Name on card: _____ Exp. date: ____ /____